EXPLORING
ethics

EXPLORING
ethics

ACTIVITY-CENTRED TEACHING TO DEVELOP THINKING ABOUT VALUES

JEREMY HAYWARD   GERALD JONES   MARILYN MASON

John Murray

© Jeremy Hayward, Gerald Jones and Marilyn Mason 2000

First published 2000
by John Murray (Publishers) Ltd
50 Albemarle Street London W1S 4BD

Reprinted 2001

Design and layouts by Geoffrey Wadsley for Aldridge Press
Illustrations by Max Ellis
Cover © Tony Stone Images
Printed and bound in Great Britain by Selwood Printing Ltd. West Sussex

A CIP record for this publication is available from the British Library

ISBN 0 7195 7181 2

Contents

Acknowledgements

The idea for this book came from conference presentations given by Jeremy Hayward and Gerald Jones. It took its first form as a collaboration with the British Humanist Association, which has always had an interest in developing moral values in education and in encouraging students to think rationally about these issues. We would like to thank the British Humanist Association for the support they have given us in putting the book together.

We are grateful to students and teachers at a number of schools, universities and colleges who have tried and tested the activities and given valuable help and feedback. In particular we would like to thank students at the University of Bristol, City and Islington College, Davies Laing and Dick College, Dulwich College, Greenford High School, the Institute of Education, Kingsway College, Mary Ward Centre, Morley College, and Orpington College. We should also like to thank Adam Morton at the University of Bristol for his valuable support and inspiration.

The environmental game, *Costing the Earth*, is based on the work of the TALESSI project team at the University of Greenwich. The team is developing resources to promote interdisciplinary, critical thinking and values awareness in environmental higher education.

About the authors

JEREMY HAYWARD is a philosophy lecturer at the Mary Ward Centre and GERALD JONES is Head of Philosophy and Religious Studies at Orpington College and Davies, Laing and Dick College. They have been teaching since 1993 and together have developed Activity-Centred Teaching as a strategy to help overcome the difficulties of teaching philosophy / ethics at A level. MARILYN MASON is Education Officer for the British Humanist Association. She has taught English, Philosophy and General Studies to secondary school students and adults.

Jeremy Hayward
jshayward@freeuk.com

Gerald Jones
geraldjones@lineone.net

Marilyn Mason
education@humanism.org.uk

Introduction

About this book

Ethics is an important part of many Advanced level subjects and growing numbers of students are expected to have grasped its key ideas and concepts. Moral issues are now on the syllabus not only of Philosophy and Religious Studies, but also of Psychology, Sociology, History, Geography, Economics, Politics, Biology, Law, Citizenship, General Studies, PSHE and Health and Social Care GNVQ.

Exploring Ethics is a resource pack for anyone teaching ethical issues. Teachers who are familiar with moral philosophy will find the activities in the book a refreshing and stimulating way of communicating ideas. Teachers who are less familiar with ethics will find that the book is an invaluable introduction to the key concepts and theories that lie behind the assumptions and intuitions of our everyday moral ideas. Vocabulary that might be unfamiliar or technical has been HIGHLIGHTED in the text on first mention and is explained in the Glossary.

As well as being an introduction to ethics, *Exploring Ethics* also offers a collection of interactive materials. We have drawn on a distinctive method of teaching moral issues – through the use of activities, exercises and games. These are aimed at stimulating intelligent discussion about moral questions and developing critical thinking skills. They will encourage students to provide reasons for supporting a point of view; to analyse theories and arguments, make hypotheses and draw inferences; to test and correct their ideas through reflection, and to develop life skills such as teamwork, co-operation and communication.

There are many ways in which *Exploring Ethics* can be used. The activities can form part of a self-contained introductory course on ethics, and the section entitled 'A Short Course on Ethics' offers ideas of how the activities could fit into such a course. Alternatively, individual games can be used to illustrate particular points that may arise in your syllabus. A ready-reference listing of the activities and the issues they cover can be found on page 21.

Activity-centred teaching

Why play games?

Ever since childhood we have played games, assumed roles and engaged in structured activities – from 'peek-a-boo' to chess, from the playground to the boardroom. As games and activities play such an important part in our lives, it is only natural that they should form a part of the learning process. Unfortunately, playing games has always been associated with the early stages of education; by secondary school they rarely see the light of day in the classroom. This is a shame: structured learning activities can be of enormous educational value, and they can provide many elements that are often lacking in traditional teaching methods.

Many educational theorists, most notably J.S. Bruner, have argued that active learning on the part of students leads to greater understanding and retention. In their book *Learning and the Simulation Game*, Taylor and Walford identify the following advantages in playing games:

- a heightened interest and excitement in learning
- a divorce from 'conventional wisdom'
- the removal of student-teacher polarisation
- learning at diverse levels
- decision-making experience
- increased empathy through role play
- a good framework for enhancing class dynamics
- a narrowing of the gap between learning and reality

These are all excellent reasons for playing educational games, but there are many more reasons still. Goodman claims that game playing is an ideal method of indirect teaching (where students learn for themselves) and should always accompany the traditional methods of direct teaching such as 'chalk and talk'. Other writers go further, for example Greenblat and Duke argue that in the future 'linear' methods of learning such as books and lectures will fail to portray the complexity of the world – only games and simulation activities will be able to do this.

There are many good reasons why we should be using games and activities in the classroom, but on a personal note, we would like to add that games can be enormously rewarding for both student and teacher. They can provide an excellent platform for future discussions, strengthen relationships in the class and make the whole educational experience fun. Have a go!

Using the activities

This book has a wide range of activities, from questionnaires, role plays and non-competitive activities, to more traditional games with scoring systems. The following points will help you make the most of the activities.

- **Educational purpose** Each of the activities is designed to explore an area of ETHICS. The next section, *A Short Course on Ethics*, links all the activities together and suggests how the activities could form part of a wider course on MORALITY. This section also helps to clarify the educational purpose of each game and gives an idea of what ethical topics they could be used to introduce, explore, or consolidate.

- **Preparation** We recommend that you read the rules through and prepare the activities in advance. All the activities come with detailed instructions as well as helpful hints and tips.

- **Materials** Some activities involve minimal equipment, such as a blank piece of paper and a pen. Others require specific materials, such as worksheets, which are provided after the rules of the game. Simply photocopy the relevant pages. Some of the games give you the option of using 'money', which can be found in Appendix 1 on pages 110–112.

- **Instructions** Try to make the instructions as clear as possible before the game begins, because if the students are unsure of the task they will switch off and not be engaged. Furthermore, it will disrupt the flow of the game if students are continually asking procedural questions.

- **Groups** The size and number of groups will vary from activity to activity, but which student is in which group should be up to you. Groups of friends may not be the most productive or interesting arrangement; a small amount of pre-planning can make the game more rewarding.

- **Competition** Some of the activities have a competitive element, which can be positive. However, if things get too competitive you may end up with self-satisfied winners and the purpose of the game forgotten. It's up to you to decide upon the degree to which competition is emphasised.

- **Adaptability** The rules of these activities are not set in stone – all of them can be adapted and changed to suit you. If an interesting point arises during a game, you may wish to discuss it there and then, or make a note of it and save it for later.

- **Practice** The more you use an activity the better it will become. Each time you will customise it slightly or remember the parts that students particularly enjoyed.

Each activity consists of instructions, other important information and, in some cases, photocopiable materials. The activities are presented in the format shown below.

Title of the activity

About the game

A brief outline of the activity.

> ### General information
>
> This is broken down into the following sections:
>
> **Length of time:** Very approximate, this can vary enormously depending on group size, etc.
>
> **Group / Class size:** Again only a suggestion, you may prefer working with different numbers.
>
> **Materials required:** Most of the materials required are provided with the relevant activities, apart from paper, pens, etc.

Aims

The educational purpose of the activity.

How to play

The instructions and rules for the activity.

Hints and tips

This section tries to pre-empt any problems you may encounter whilst using the game. It also includes suggestions for variations on the activities.

Points for discussion

Ideas on how to draw out interesting points from the activity into classroom discussions.

Philosophical background

Not every activity includes this section. It is included for those instances where you need to understand some of the philosophy that lies behind the activity. Further background is provided in the Glossary, page 102.

A Short Course on Ethics

The activities have been divided into groups according to which aspects of ethics they touch on. This table illustrates the overall scope and structure of the course.

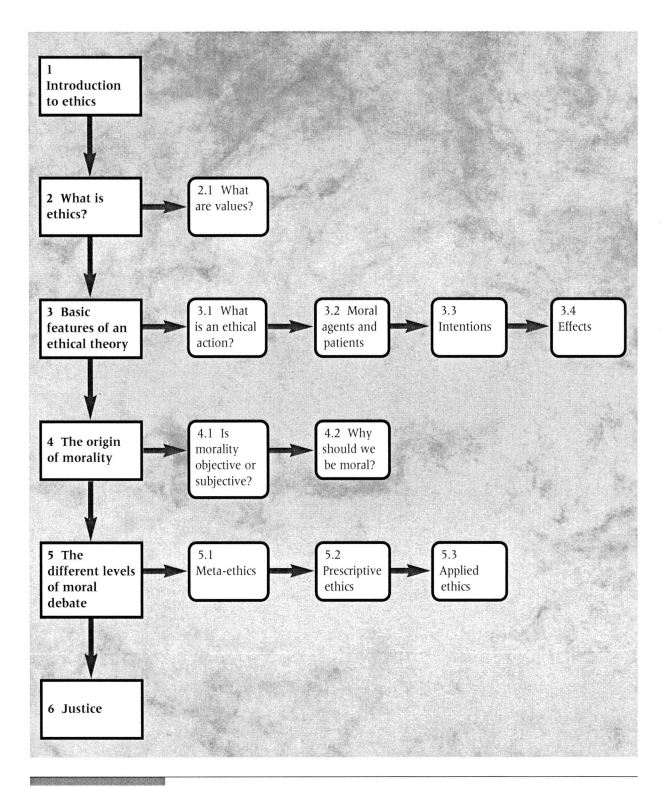

1 Introduction to ethics

Moral debates dominate the media: stories about the private lives of politicians, euthanasia, the atrocities of war, concerns about the environment, drugs and abortion cover the front pages of the national press every day. Such contemporary issues are a staple part of PSHE courses, and students are encouraged to air their views and freely discuss such subjects.

However, all too often classroom discussions do not move beyond the level of 'This is my opinion, what's yours?' Such expressions of belief, valuable though they may be, are only one small aspect of ethical debates and they often leave both teacher and students dissatisfied, with students talking at cross-purposes and on different levels. A more critical approach to ethical thinking is needed – moral philosophy provides such an approach.

For thousands of years philosophers have questioned our ordinary beliefs. The best thinkers have done this by inviting us to reflect actively on our beliefs: What are our beliefs based on? Are they contradictory? What assumptions are we making? What hidden prejudices do we have? The purpose of such reflection in ethics is to arrive at a moral theory that is justifiable, free from inconsistencies, and in which the presuppositions are there for all to see.

This course attempts to stretch the minds of those interested in moral questions through active engagement with the relevant issues. The aims of the course are for students to come to a clearer understanding of the following:

■ how moral judgements are made
■ what kinds of moral beliefs and theories there are
■ moral concepts such as good / bad, right / wrong, MORAL AGENT / MORAL PATIENT
■ different levels of moral debate

2 What is ethics?

One way of understanding ethics (or moral philosophy) is to look at the kinds of question it tries to answer:

- Is the deforestation of the Amazon wrong?
- Should we carry out research on cloned embryos?
- Why should politicians tell the truth?
- Can euthanasia ever be for the good?

What do ethical questions have in common? Whereas science tries to describe the world as it is, and history how it was, ethical questions are concerned with how we *ought* to live and how we *should* act. In particular, ethics is concerned with human goodness and with how we can achieve such goodness through our actions.

There are many ways we can choose to live our lives. We could try to make as much money as possible; we could marry, get a mortgage, retire then die; or we could be kind to animals, think only of others and fight for a cause we believe in. But which is the right way to live our lives? There are many different responses to this question – reflected in the many different religions, cultures, races, creeds and philosophies throughout the world. What distinguishes moral philosophy from other ethical systems is the way that philosophers try to question all our assumptions and beliefs. It is an approach that forces us to think about our reasons for living and acting as we do. According to SOCRATES, this is one of the most important things we can do, because 'an unexamined life is not worth living'.

We will begin our examination by exploring the issue of *values*. Many people claim that it is our values, the things we desire most, that provide our ultimate reasons for acting as we do. Other people claim that those actions we call *good* and *bad* are simply reflections of what society finds valuable.

2.1 What are values?

Activities THE WORLD'S MOST VALUABLE THING [page 22]
THE END GAME [page 24]
THE IDEAL LIFE EXHIBITION [page 29]

The things we value are revealed in the choices we make. If we were to follow someone for a year, we would soon learn the kinds of things they considered important – the things they desire. They might regularly attend a gym – thus revealing that they value their health or their looks; they might be out on the town every night – they value their friends; they might read on their way to work – they value knowledge, or the pleasures of fiction.

ARISTOTLE claimed that, without exception, all our actions are done with some goal in mind. Even apparently pointless actions have a purpose and are aimed at something that we want, something we value. So values, far from being an abstract ideal, are operating on our daily lives all the time. *The End Game* aims to illustrate this point.

What things do we value? If you were given absolute control over your existence and told to create your perfect life, then you would include everything that you valued – material goods, relationships, your inner life and your hopes for the world around you. *The Ideal Life Exhibition* invites students to do just this. It highlights the fact that everyone, even the most cynical of students, has values.

What makes something valuable? *The World's Most Valuable Thing* asks students to compare things of different value: personal, global, environmental, aesthetic and material. In doing so, students have to provide reasons why they think that one thing is valuable and another thing is not, or why one is more valuable than another. Are some things intrinsically valuable, or is everything valuable simply because it is useful? Learning to justify a belief by offering reasons for it is an essential part of ethical and critical thinking.

How are values linked to morality? As a general rule, if a society values particular things, for example dogs, then harming dogs would be considered bad in that society. We may conclude that when an action harms something that is valued then it is usually called *bad*; when an action promotes something that is valued then it is called *good*. Other philosophers have argued that morality should not be linked to material values, and that the moral realm is distinct from this world.

3 Basic features of an ethical theory

Ethics, unlike many other parts of philosophy, is a practical as well as a theoretical subject. It begins with the choices and dilemmas we face in the real world, but tries to move beyond these concrete problems to construct general theories about our actions and judgements. This section is concerned with examining the basic features that characterise most ethical theories: action, AGENCY, intention and effects. We shall see in a later section the different emphases philosophers have given to these features in constructing their ethical systems.

3.1 What is an ethical action?

Activity THE M.O.R.A.L. QUESTIONNAIRE [page 32]

We have seen how all of our actions are shaped by values, but the question we must now address is 'What is it that makes an action an ethical one?'

Some of our actions are not considered to be ethical at all (they are neither good nor bad), whereas other actions are. Sharpening a pencil or counting apples are neither good nor bad acts, in isolation they are morally neutral. Stealing from schools or helping the disadvantaged are considered moral actions (one bad, the other one good).

However, what makes an act enter the moral arena? In other words, what features of actions such as stealing or being charitable make us judge them to be good or bad, right or wrong? Whether or not we are aware of it, we all have our own gut-feelings about this subject; we have been brought up to see some actions as ethically significant and others as morally neutral. We pass moral judgement on the former (we call them good or bad), we ignore the latter.

It is common practice in philosophy to delineate concepts by drawing up criteria that define the concept. If we want to know what makes an action ethical, then we should arrive at some criteria that help us to distinguish between moral actions and morally neutral actions. *The M.O.R.A.L. Questionnaire* is a method of bringing out students' own moral opinions about this distinction and it serves as an excellent introduction to any ethical discussion.

The key criteria of moral acts, ones that distinguish them from morally neutral acts, might be summarised as follows:

- Moral acts are performed by AGENTS: creatures that are capable of free choice.
- Moral acts are the result of intention: the action was done on purpose and the agent is aware of what they are doing and is acting deliberately. Some unintentional acts can also be moral, such as those committed, or failing to be committed, through negligence. The general rule is that moral acts must be intentional; accidents are not usually considered to be moral.
- Moral acts have a significant effect on PATIENTS: these consequences tend to be significant in the amount of harm or benefit they bring to others.

We will now explore each of these criteria in more detail.

3.2 Moral agents and patients

Activities

THE THING FROM PLANET Z [page 36]
DRAWING THE LINE [page 44]

What distinguishes the items in each of these pairs?

A meteor hits the Earth, destroying a city.	A biochemical bomb hits the Earth destroying a city.
A tigress rips the throat of a baby elephant.	A poacher rips the throat of a baby elephant.
A hurricane fells all the trees in a tropical rain forest.	A multinational corporation fells all the trees in a tropical rain forest.

In each pair the physical damage and pain caused is the same, so why do we judge the first set of cases as morally neutral and the second as morally wrong? One reason is that the scenarios in the first column do not seem to involve any deliberate choice, they were all the results of natural processes. Having the capacity to make deliberate acts (whatever that involves) seems a necessary condition for moral action. We call beings with such a capacity MORAL AGENTS.

Two interconnected questions arise here:

■ Firstly, what determines whether or not a creature is a moral agent? Is it that it is capable of free choice, or that it is self-aware, or that it possesses a soul, or that it has a moral conscience?

■ Secondly, how can we tell whether or not a creature is a moral agent? If ARTIFICIAL INTELLIGENCE continues progressing for the next hundred years at the rate it is now, then we may eventually have to decide whether computers are moral agents.

Imagine we encounter an alien species, or discover new facts about a species on Earth, then we may have to alter our view that only humans are capable of moral decisions. These issues are explored in *The Thing from Planet Z*, which invites students to draw up their own criteria as to what makes something a moral agent.

We can see that the concept of a moral agent is important in deciding whether an action is ethical. However, we should not only consider who is doing the act but also who is on the receiving end of the act. Take, for example, the action of stamping on something. If it were a rock, or some other inanimate object then we would probably say the action was morally neutral, if it were a cuddly animal our judgement would change. But what about killing ants, flies or single cell organisms? In *Drawing the Line* and *The Thing from Planet Z* students have the opportunity to determine what sort of creature they consider to be a MORAL PATIENT and worthy of moral respect.

3.3 Intentions

Activity

MORAL DILEMMAS [page 47]
UNIVERSALISABILITY CHALLENGE [page 65]

It is common sense to view accidental actions differently from deliberate actions. *Moral Dilemmas* explores our intuition that moral acts are the result of intention: if I accidentally tread on your toe, then apologise, I guess you would say I had done nothing wrong. However, if I deliberately grind my heel into your foot, you would say that I had done something morally wrong, no matter how profuse my apology.

We may all agree that intentions are important to morality but some philosophers, for example, KANT (see 5.2, page 16ff) have gone further and claimed they are the only relevant features of a moral act. According to this view an act should be judged to be right or wrong solely by the motives behind the act. Whether such theories are true or not, intentions are certainly fundamental to our ordinary moral judgements. *Moral Dilemmas* can be used to show how it is possible to judge an act by the intention of the person committing it *Universalisability Challenge* deals specifically with Kant's theory of ethics.

3.4 Effects

Activity

MORAL DILEMMAS [page 47]
HEALTH OR WEALTH? [page 70]

There are, however, many actions that may be judged good or bad irrespective of the original motives. If I intend to save the world and end up destroying it, then we may want to say that my action was a bad one because it resulted in the deaths of seven billion people. Consequences, just as much as motives, are part of the fabric of our moral beliefs.

In general we say that if an action has beneficial consequences (either because it generates happiness or prevents harm) then it is a good action; if an action produces detrimental effects then it is a bad action. There are many problems associated with this theory: how do we measure or predict the benefits or harm an act brings? When do the consequences of an act come to an end? These problems are mentioned again in 5.2 on page 16 where we look at the theory of UTILITARIANISM, and in *Health or Wealth?* where students apply utilitarianism to a variety of medical dilemmas.

We have now sketched some of the basic features of a moral theory. They are concerned with actions that affect others (moral patients), and are deliberate and performed by an agent. These ideas do not sit happily alongside one another, and in particular there is a direct conflict between those who see good intentions as essential to a good act, and those who see good consequences as essential. The examples we have given in *Moral Dilemmas* bring out this conflict and invite students to consider which feature they consider to be most important in morality.

4 The origin of morality

Our students ask us time and again, 'Where do morals come from?' Are moral laws 'out there' in the world, waiting to be discovered like the laws of nature? Or is morality a matter of personal opinion or social conditioning? This distinction between things that are 'out there' (like scientific facts) and those that are 'inside me' (like personal taste) is nicely captured by the concepts of *objective* and *subjective*. Is morality objective or subjective? Did humans invent it, or does it exist independently of humans?

The majority of people think that morality is objective, it exists independently of human beings. The United Nations estimates that there are between three to four billion people who are religious, and most religions hold that morality transcends humans – it is the creation of God/s. Are religious believers right? Many would claim that morality is not possible without God. They would claim that:

- If there is no God, then morality is neither absolute nor objective. It loses its claim over our actions.
- If there is no God, then why should we be moral at all? As Dostoyevsky wrote in *The Brothers Karamazov*, 'If God is dead, everything is permitted.'
- If there is no God, then how can we explain the stable and moral nature of society?

It is true that religious belief is the foundation for many people's notion of morality. But it is also one of the central tenets of humanism, and of modern philosophy in general, that we are able to justify, support and utilise morality just as successfully by excluding religion as by assuming it. If we deny that morality is based on religion, does that make morality purely subjective?

4.1 Is morality objective or subjective?

This question of the status of morality is an important one. We might summarise the answers to the question 'Where does morality come from?' in the following three ways:

1 It is objective There is an absolute moral law, independent of a human perspective, that dictates what we should and shouldn't do. In other words morality is more than just a matter of opinion. Some questions, such as 'Is ice-cream better than chocolate?' have no definite answer, only various opinions. Whereas other questions such as 'What is 2+3?' do have absolute answers. People who claim that morality is objective are claiming that moral questions such as 'Is it ever right to steal?' also have absolute answers (although sometimes we might not know what they are). Such people usually hold one of the following positions:

■ God made the moral law, and has revealed it to us in the form of commandments; it is up to us to follow these commands. Some believers claim we should follow the commandments to the letter, others that they need reinterpreting as we encounter new moral problems.

■ The moral law is a part of the fabric of the universe, and even God/s are subject to it. Some philosophers, for example Kant, think that this moral law is discoverable by reason. Others think that humans have a special sense that helps us detect what is right or wrong; some call this a *moral intuition*, others call it a *moral conscience*.

2 It is subjective There is no such thing as an absolute morality. Moral questions have no absolute answers only various opinions. People who believe this could hold one of many positions:

■ Morality is down to the individual, it is something they decide for themselves. What I think is right, is right 'for me'; and what you think is right, is right 'for you'. Such an extreme subjective position can mean that moral discussion and argument becomes impossible, and as pointless as trying to persuade someone who hates cabbage that deep down they really like it.

■ Morality is the product of socialisation. Every society has its own morality, and therefore *good* and *bad* refer to different kinds of actions in different societies (also a form of RELATIVISM). Morality is simply the set of rules that enables each society to remain stable and run smoothly – the cynic might claim that it is actually only those in power who benefit from these moral rules. A slightly more positive account might be that everyone in society benefits from a moral upbringing, and without it we might be tearing each other apart.

■ Morality is the result of biological or genetic factors. Individuals have evolved in such a way that we perform a certain amount of seemingly altruistic, selfless acts. Such behaviour we call *good*. Thinkers who argue along these lines suggest that the real origin of ethics lies in the way we have evolved as social animals.

The theory that all moral and value judgements are dependent upon the individual or society is known as relativism. A relativist would claim that there is no absolute answer to questions such as 'Who's better: Beethoven or the Beatles?' or 'What's worse: killing whales or killing humans?'

3 It is intersubjective This word is used by philosophers to describe something that is not quite objective, but nor is it purely subjective, it falls in the middle ground between the two. Moral questions may not have absolute answers, but they are more than just opinion.

■ To say that morality is intersubjective is to say that it is commonly agreed that some actions are good and some bad. By 'commonly agreed' we mean that there are conventions agreed on by nearly everyone, but that these conventions do not refer to something that exists beyond human beings; indeed these conventions may change over time. How and why intersubjective moral rules, such as 'Tell the truth', 'Do not harm innocent persons', 'Respect promises and contracts', 'Do not break taboos', come about is a matter for debate; but it seems that they exist in a general form in all societies. Some people have argued that it is down to evolution: societies and individuals that abide by these rules tend to survive, and those societies that don't become unstable and disintegrate.

The status of moral beliefs is still a matter of debate and is dependent upon other beliefs we have about the universe. The answer we give to this issue will influence another very important question, 'Why should we be moral?'

4.2 Why should we be moral?

Activities

ARE YOU A HUMANIST? [page 55]
THE PRISONER'S DILEMMA [page 60]

Some people think that we have a duty to do good, some would claim that it is in our best interests to be good. Some people have no desire to be moral at all. The question 'Why should we be moral?' is a difficult one to answer and largely depends on where we think morality comes from. The *Are You a Humanist?* questionnaire asks students to examine their own beliefs, and in particular reveals whether they believe the source of morality is God or humanity.

Here are some common explananations for why we should be moral:

■ We will be rewarded either spiritually or materially:
We may be spiritually rewarded either in this life or the next (as a result of karma, or of the judgement of God/s). Perhaps we will just feel better or be happier if we do the right thing.
    We may be materially rewarded by society for good moral behaviour. This clearly isn't always the case – but the hope of reward can provide some motivation.

■ We are afraid of spiritual or material punishment:
Spiritual punishment may be in this life or in the next; by God or by karmic forces, or simply by feeling guilty or unhappy.
    Material or social punishment comes in the form of things most of us wish to avoid, such as social exclusion, prison or execution.

■ We want to be moral. This may be because of our genetic make-up, or because we have an innate moral sense, or because we want to please God.

■ We are socially DETERMINED to be moral. It is in society's interest that we are moral, and so we are conditioned or educated so that we generally behave in a moral way. By the time we are adults we are socially determined, and we don't have much choice about changing our behaviour patterns.

■ It is in our own best interests to be moral. Even if we accept that humans are naturally selfish, we can still argue that the most beneficial form of selfishness is, paradoxically, selflessness. In other words, we will do best for ourselves if we behave in a moral way towards others.

The Prisoner's Dilemma illustrates how it is possible to be a MATERIALIST, i.e. without any belief in God or anything transcendental, and yet still offer good reasons to be moral.

5 The different levels of moral debate

As we mentioned earlier, there are many different levels of ethical debate that can easily become confused. You may have noticed that in heated pub-style ethical debates people often seem to be talking at cross-purposes, on different levels. One person may be arguing that abortion is wrong, another may argue that utilitarianism is wrong, a third may claim that morality doesn't exist, saying it's all a load of hot air. They do not seem to be engaging on the same level. This is because there are several different ways in which we can talk about morality.

Philosophers tend to divide ethics into three distinct levels of debate. We have left this topic towards the end of the course because it really concerns 'fine-tuning' classroom discussion, and it may be something that only older students will grasp.

The three levels of ethics can be illustrated by looking at the different ways a philosopher might respond to the question 'Is it ever morally permissible to kill an innocent person?' There might be three responses:

1 On the level of meta-ethics we might analyse the question or the concepts.
2 On the level of PRESCRIPTIVE ETHICS we may look at a whole system of morality and the judgements it makes about what makes things good or bad in general.
3 On the level of APPLIED ETHICS we look at the application of a prescriptive theory to a real-life issue.

5.1 Meta-ethics

Activities ARE YOU A HUMANIST? [page 55]
THE PRISONER'S DILEMMA [page 60]
THE THING FROM PLANET Z [page 36]

Meta-ethics involves defining and coming to an agreement about the key concepts involved in moral discussion. It requires standing back from the actual debate and sorting out what the ground rules are. Let's think then about the question 'Is it ever morally permissible to kill an innocent person?'

It is crucial for those who wish to answer this question that they first discuss what is meant by *person* – is a dolphin a person? Is a two-day-old embryo or a fetus a person? Do 'persons' command a special moral position; for example, should we respect the sanctity of their lives? *The Thing from Planet Z* is an exercise in making a meta-ethical distinction between beings that are moral patients and those that are not.

What is meant by *innocent*? Many would say that it is not wrong to kill enemy soldiers in war, partly because soldiers are not innocent. Some would say that capital punishment is not wrong, because criminals are not innocent. Are there degrees of innocence?

What is meant by *morally permissible*? Some modern philosophers have claimed that words like *good* and *bad* mean 'I approve (or do not approve) of this kind of behaviour', in other words, they are totally subjective judgements. Some have claimed that *good* means 'done in accordance with God's law', whilst others have a rational definition of goodness.

So the meaning of moral terms needs to be discussed. It is also important that the origins of morality are discussed. If by *moral* you mean 'done in accordance with the word of God' then this must be made clear to someone who thinks that *moral* means 'whatever society agrees is moral'.

The Prisoner's Dilemma and the *Are You a Humanist?* questionnaire raise meta-ethical questions about the meaning and foundations of moral discussion.

5.2 Prescriptive ethics

Activities UNIVERSALISABILITY CHALLENGE [page 65]
HEALTH OR WEALTH? [page 70]

Prescriptive or normative ethics is the level on which most people debate morality. At this level we are concerned with trying to arrive at and justify some of the rules that we think should determine people's behaviour. In other words, we are prescribing certain kinds of behaviour, setting a norm: we are saying what people should and shouldn't do, and why they should or shouldn't do it. When discussing prescriptive ethics, philosophers are looking at what kinds of actions are good or bad, right or wrong and they may put forward and debate whole systems of ethics (such as utilitarianism, Christian ethics, or Kantian ethics).

All moral theories tend to fall into one of four main types:

1 CONSEQUENTIALIST For a consequentialist, such as JOHN STUART MILL (a utilitarian) a good action is one that brings about good consequences, and all other features of the action are irrelevant. For utilitarians what is important about the consequences of a good act is that they minimise pain and maximise happiness. *Health or Wealth?* is an excellent simulation of this way of thinking as students are asked to put aside their moral intuitions and prejudices and judge the situations on the consequences alone.

2 ABSOLUTIST For an absolutist, it is the action itself, not the consequences or motive, that is important. Some actions are simply good, and some are simply bad. The moral codes of the major religions, and in particular The Ten Commandments, are good illustrations of this kind of moral thinking.

3 *Motivist* For a motivist it is neither the action itself, nor the consequences that are good, but solely the intention with which it was done. So a good action is one done from good motives. Immanuel Kant thought that the only truly good motive was that of DUTY. *Universalisability Challenge* illustrates this aspect of Kant's moral theory.

4 *Agent-centred ethics* A few philosophers, most famously in Ancient Greece, focused not on the action but on the agent performing the action. For them, *good* referred to the person, not to the action. PLATO and Aristotle both had very strong views on what makes someone good. This kind of theory emphasises education and the development of character.

The relationship between these four prescriptive theories can be illustrated in the following way:

Exploring Ethics   © JOHN MURRAY

AGENT-CENTRED ETHICS	ACT-CENTRED ETHICS		
	Motivism	Absolutism	Consequentialism
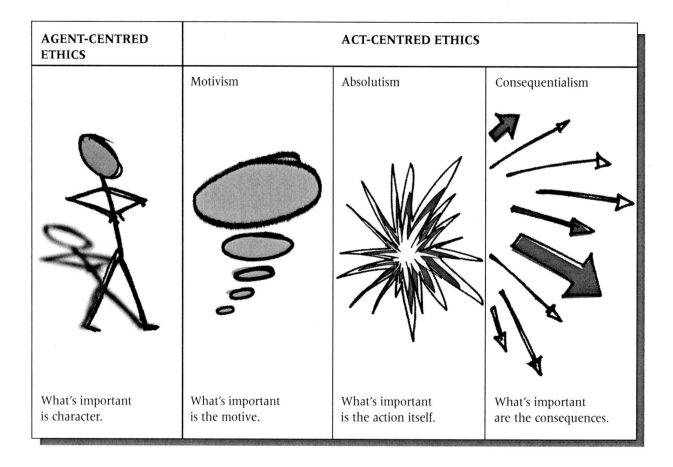			
What's important is character.	What's important is the motive.	What's important is the action itself.	What's important are the consequences.

5.3 Applied ethics

Activities

MORAL DILEMMAS [page 47]
UNIVERSALISABILITY CHALLENGE [page 65]
HEALTH OR WEALTH? [page 70]
COSTING THE EARTH [page 79]

Whether you believe that morality stems from God (meta-ethics), whether you feel that your religion is the best general guide for behaviour (prescriptive ethics), or whether you think that morality is a human creation, you will still be left with ethical dilemmas. For example, sacred texts are not specific on issues such as whether cloning is right, or whether genetically modified soya beans should be grown. Human societies and laws often lag behind scientific developments. We are still left with the problem of how to apply ethical theories to actual situations in the world. This is the domain of applied ethics.

At this level of applied ethics (sometimes called PRACTICAL ETHICS), we examine how an ethical theory such as utilitarianism can be applied to situations in the real world. It is this type of problem that students often enjoy the most, as it requires getting involved with the nitty-gritty of contemporary moral dilemmas. It can also lead to the most emotionally charged discussions, as students find themselves having to question and defend their own beliefs about controversial issues.

Applying a theory to a moral dilemma can be enlightening, for it is here that we find the limits of our own intuitions and the usefulness of having an ethical theory. *Health or Wealth?* and *Universalisability Challenge* expose some of the strengths and weaknesses of putting an ethical theory into practice. By engaging in practical ethics in this way we discover some of the major problems within ethical theories. In particular, reflecting on the application of theory to practice can

■ bring out many of the problems and contradictions within the moral theory itself.
■ lead to criticisms of and alteration of that theory.
■ reveal inconsistencies in students' thoughts, for example – why is abortion morally permissible and yet infanticide not; is it merely a question of living outside of the womb?
■ lead us to reflect on our own moral beliefs – are they coherent? Are they bound by one moral theory, or are there several we hold, each having priority in different situations?

As an introduction to practical ethics, students can attempt to solve the *Moral Dilemmas*, whereby they apply differing prescriptive theories to problematic situations. But these simple examples are only indicative of the sorts of issues that students could discuss, and they lack the complexity of genuine contemporary debates about the following, for example:

■ euthanasia
■ the arms trade
■ animal rights
■ abortion
■ eugenics and genetic research
■ the environment

Some of these issues are addressed in these activities, for example, environmental issues are debated in *Costing the Earth*. Students should find themselves better equipped to think clearly and talk about other contemporary ethical issues after engaging in the activities.

So we can see that there are three different levels on which ethics can be debated, and it is important to distinguish clearly between them. Differences of opinion over a prescriptive ethical system may result from disagreements about the origin of ethics; and disagreements over solutions to contemporary moral dilemmas may arise because of differences over the ethical system to be used.

6 Justice

Justice and politics are two topics that are closely connected to ethics. If ethics is seen as trying to answer the question 'How should I live my life?' then politics can be seen as an attempt to answer the question 'How should we live our lives together?' Justice is the bridge between ethics and politics. It is concerned with the ethics of who in society should receive the benefits and who should carry the burdens. This is known as *distributive justice*. It is also concerned with who should be punished and who rewarded, and how this should be done. This is known as *corrective justice*.

Many students have a strong sense of justice and injustice. From a very early age children can be heard to cry 'That's not fair!' Films and dramas often tap into our intuitive sense of justice. However, most students will not have thought about what justice actually is or about where their sense of justice comes from. There is a cluster of activities included in the book that help students to explore their own ideas of justice.

Planet Thera offers students a chance to explore their own ideas of what a just society would be like. The game can make the students consider how they would distribute benefits and burdens amongst a group of stranded humans. It brings out the students' intuitions about justice and can be used as a platform to discuss many different issues.

There Are No Laws enables students to consider how society would behave if punishments did not exist. It can also encourage students to explore their philosophical relationship with the law.

Just a Minute introduces students to different ideas about justice, but it is primarily designed to sharpen students' critical thinking by encouraging them to think about the nature of arguments. The game is based on the beginning of Plato's masterpiece, the *Republic*, and sees Socrates dismissing several concepts of justice. *Socrateaser* follows on from this, enabling students to follow in the footsteps of Socrates and analyse moral concepts themselves.

Activities for Exploring Ethics

The next section of the book contains the sixteen activities, exercises and games. This chart shows the main issues covered by the activities.

ACTIVITY	ISSUES COVERED	PAGE
1 The World's Most Valuable Thing	Values in general	22
2 The End Game	What reasons lie behind our actions?	24
3 The Ideal Life Exhibition	What sort of life do we want?	29
4 The M.O.R.A.L. Questionnaire	What makes an issue a *moral* issue?	32
5 The Thing from Planet Z	When it comes to morality, are humans different from other animals?	36
6 Drawing the Line	Which animals are morally significant? When is it OK to harm animals?	44
7 Moral Dilemmas	Solving moral dilemmas Putting ethics into practice	47
8 Are You a Humanist?	Can we have values without God?	55
9 The Prisoner's Dilemma	Is co-operation the basis of morality? Where do morals come from?	60
10 Universalisability Challenge	What happens if everyone acts like that? Putting Kant's ethics into practice	65
11 Health or Wealth?	Medical ethics Putting utilitarianism into practice	70
12 Costing the Earth	Environmental ethics	79
13 Planet Thera	What sort of society would we like to live in?	82
14 There Are No Laws	What would life be like without morality?	87
15 Just a Minute	Developing critical thinking A taster of Plato on justice	89
16 Socrateaser	How to argue (in the tradition of Socrates)	98

1 The World's Most Valuable Thing

About the game

A short, enjoyable questionnaire designed to explore the students' personal values. A very good starting point for further discussions.

General information

Length of time: 15–30 minutes
Group / class size: 1–6 students per group, class size unlimited
Materials required: *The World's Most Valuable Thing* (WMVT) form

---

Aims

To encourage students to explore their values and try to see what makes something valuable.

How to play

1   Divide the class into groups. Give each group a copy of the WMVT form.
2   Ask the students to complete the form by picking the most valuable thing in each group. These six items progress to the semi-finals, and now students should pick the two most valuable items, one from each new group.
3   The final reveals what each group considers to be the most valuable thing.

Hints and tips

■ Ask students to write down their reasons for picking each item. What makes each item more valuable?

■ For a further exercise, or for students who finish early, you could ask them what values are missing? Students should think of things that they believe would make it through to the semi-finals.

Points for discussion

■ How do values relate to ethics? Invite students to think of a list of good and bad actions; students should think about how the good actions could be seen as contributing towards something we value, and how the bad actions could be seen as damaging something we value.

■ Ask students to consider how people in different cultures and countries may have different values, and thus a different morality.

■ What makes something valuable? Can anything be inherently valuable (valuable in itself)? Or does value come from rarity or uniqueness? Many philosophers would say that we value things for their UTILITY – in other words because they promote happiness or benefit society in some way.

STUDENT'S PAGE

The World's Most Valuable Thing

WMVT

It's that time again when, with hushed breath, the nation watches the media event of the decade. The most treasured things from around the world will be represented as the battle commences to become the WMVT! You have been asked to sit on the panel that awards this prestigious prize – it is your job to choose from each section what you personally think is most valuable. By the end of the night there will be tears, there will be tantrums, there will be laughter and there will be joy, but above all there will be a winner! You and your fellow panellists will find the WORLD'S MOST VALUABLE THING!

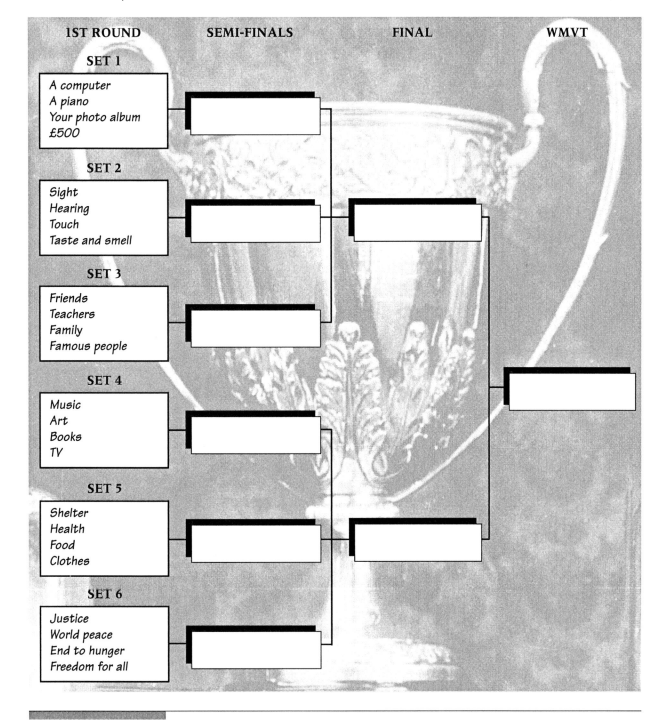

1ST ROUND	SEMI-FINALS	FINAL	WMVT

SET 1
A computer
A piano
Your photo album
£500

SET 2
Sight
Hearing
Touch
Taste and smell

SET 3
Friends
Teachers
Family
Famous people

SET 4
Music
Art
Books
TV

SET 5
Shelter
Health
Food
Clothes

SET 6
Justice
World peace
End to hunger
Freedom for all

Exploring Ethics © JOHN MURRAY

2 The End Game

About the game

A short exercise designed to examine what are our goals in life, and whether there is an ultimate goal that we are all striving for.

General information

Length of time: 20–25 minutes (15 minutes for the exercise, 10 minutes for feedback)

Group / Class size: Involves the whole class, class size 5–20 students

Materials required: A blank piece of paper and pen for each student

Aims

To show that everything we do has a purpose and is based on a value that we hold.

How to play

1 **Round One** – Students write their names at the top of a blank piece of paper. Below that they should write:

I attend college in order to ...

and they should complete the sentence by thinking about their reason for attending college. For example:

I attend college in order to take my A levels.

2 **Round Two** – Students then pass their piece of paper to the person on their left. Each student should now take the end of the previous sentence and use it to begin a new sentence. For example:

I take my A levels in order to ...

Students should complete this sentence, explaining for example:

I take my A levels in order to go to university.

3 **Round Three** – When the second sentence has been completed, students should fold over the first sentence, so that only the second sentence is visible, and once again pass it to the person on their left.

4 Repeat this process so that in each round every student receives a piece of paper with one sentence visible, uses the end of that sentence to construct a new sentence, completes the new sentence, folds the paper so that only this new sentence is visible, and passes it to their left.

The exercise should continue for about seven or eight rounds, or until the students can no longer think of a reason, for example:

I want to be happy in order to ... ???

5   Students return the papers back to the person whose name is at the top, and you should invite students to read them aloud (particularly if they are funny or insightful).

6   In a feedback session, clarify the distinction between means and ends (see *Philosophical background* below) and discuss the reasons why we do things. You might go further in exploring whether there is one final goal that all human activities are aimed at: perhaps happiness, or pleasure, or spiritual enlightenment, or moral perfection.

Hints and tips

■   Alternatively, students can simply write out a list of means and ends themselves without passing the list round. As this version is quicker, students could think of their own starting points in order to work out their ultimate end. For example:

I buy shaving foam in order to ...
I go to the party in order to ...
I chew gum in order to ...
I read newspapers in order to ...

Asking students to do several of these chains allows you to explore whether all actions are aimed at one particular end, or whether there are several ends our actions are aimed at (see *The Ideal Life Exhibition*, page 29).

■   Students might have to rephrase the end of the previous sentence by placing 'I want to ...' in front of it. This will make their sentence more meaningful, and it is worth saying this to students at the start. For example, instead of writing 'to pass my A levels' it makes more sense to write 'I want to pass my A levels in order to ...'

■   Students should be thinking of the goals, not the causes of their actions, so they must avoid writing 'because' instead of 'in order to'. For example the sentence 'I attend college because I got my grant cheque this morning' misses the point of the exercise because it reveals nothing about the intentions of the student only about the efficiency of the postal service!

■   Be prepared for a wide range of reasons for doing things. A finished piece of paper might look like this:

> I attend college in order to take A levels.
>
> I take A levels in order to go to university.
>
> I go to university in order to please my parents.
>
> I want to please my parents in order to have an easy life at home.
>
> I want to have an easy life at home in order to stay there for ever and have no responsibilities.
>
> I want to stay at home for ever without responsibilities in order to have an easy life.
>
> I want to have an easy life in order to ...

Apparently the ultimate point of attending college is to have an easy life! Note how in this example the reasons given became circular: the students perceive having an easy life not as means to some future end, but as an end in itself.

■ Although we have suggested 'I attend college ...' as a starting point (because it brings home the importance of education), this need not be the starting point for every class. 'I walk down the road in order to ...' is a sentence that allows students' imagination full rein, but any activity will do.

Points for discussion

■ Does every action have a purpose? The exercise seems to imply that everything does, but is it possible to think of something that humans do that is not done for a purpose? You should invite students to think of counter-examples, activities that seem to have no purpose (e.g. fidgeting, doodling whilst on the phone, or switching a light on and off repeatedly). The question then is: are these genuine counter-examples? Anyone with a theory of the subconscious may be able to account for all behaviour, even so-called irrational kinds, by reference to subconscious desires and goals.

■ What does this have to do with morality? The exercise reveals something strikingly obvious: that every one of us has values (that we may or may not be aware of) and these values determine or guide our behaviour. The question then to ask students is should they have the values that their actions betray, for example *should* they be seeking pleasure over and above everything else? Now that is a big ethical issue: what should we be seeking to do in our time on this Earth – how should we live our lives?

Philosophical background

What is the distinction between a MEANS, an END, and an END-IN-ITSELF?

Means Much of what we do is simply a step on the way to some other future activity, it helps us achieve that future, it helps us to get there; that is what is understood by *means*.

End Very often it is the future activity or process that we are really aiming at, this is what is understood by *end*. So, for example, I may put the kettle on (means) to make a cup of tea (end). Some ends are also means to another goal, and the exercise brings this out, as it reveals a chain of means and ends that serve some further end. In this example, drinking the tea might be a means to staying awake, or quenching my thirst.

End-in-itself If, however, the end is done for its own sake then it is an *end-in-itself*. For many people there is no further reason for having a nice cup of tea, it is just good to have one. Many philosophers and psychologists have argued that the only true end-in-itself, the only thing we ultimately aim at for its own sake, is pleasure. In this exercise students may find that in some cases it doesn't make sense to give a reason or ask why, e.g. 'I want to be happy in order to ...' This is an indication that such things are ends-in-themselves, done for their own sake.

How can we achieve our goals? In the *Ethics*, Aristotle discussed the ideal life and how it was possible to attain this life. He analysed human action and argued that every single thing we do is aimed at some end; moreover, he claimed that there was one thing that we all wanted and that was to lead the Good Life. The way to reach this Good Life was to flourish as a human being and in particular to use our reason. Aristotle argued that there was one particular use of reason that would help us reach our goals and this was working backwards from these goals to the situation we are in at the moment. In order to achieve our goal we simply follow the path we have created.

Here is an example: let us say that the Silhouette Student's goal is to be happy, the question is how does she get there?

GOAL

Happiness

Perhaps the one single thing that will make a difference to her will be job satisfaction, so this must be the step she needs to reach before she reaches happiness.

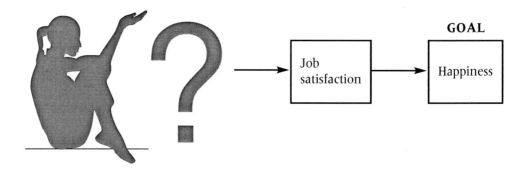

She should then ask herself what she needs to get job satisfaction. A set of good transferable skills might be one thing.

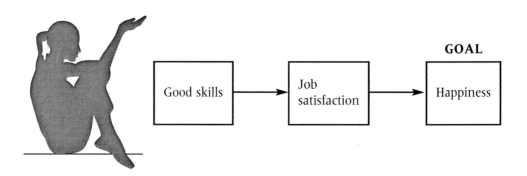

In order to get good skills she needs to work hard at university, in order to do that she needs to pass her A levels ..., etc.

By reasoning in this way, we create a chain of intermediary goals until we arrive at the first step, which is something we can do in the situation we are in now, i.e. to do your homework whilst at college.

3 The Ideal Life Exhibition

About the game

Students are invited to outline a vision of their ideal life.

General information

Length of time: 20–25 minutes (15 minutes for the exercise, 10 minutes for feedback)

Group / Class size: Students work individually, class size unlimited

Materials required: A blank piece of paper and pen for each student

---

Aims

To enable students to consider what they want from life and whether there is an ultimate goal that we are all striving for.

How to play

Stage One – The purpose of this stage is for students to indulge themselves in the kind of life they would like to lead, and to share their vision with the rest of the class if they so wish.

Students draw the following table on a blank sheet of paper:

THE IDEAL LIFE

1 Material objects	2 Physical attributes	3 Mental attributes
4 Relationships	5 Achievements / experiences	6 Environment

Students write under each of these headings the things that would be a part of their ideal life. What material objects (including money) would they have? What would they be like physically (health and appearance)? What mental, emotional or psychological characteristics would they have? What relationships would they like to have? What would they like to do in their ideal life? And finally what would the world around them be like?

Go round the class asking students what they have put in each category. Some of these can be written on the board so that students can share their ideal life with other class members.

Stage Two – The purpose of this stage is for students to think about why they have chosen the things on the list. What do they value in life, and how do the things they have chosen help them attain these values? (You may already be familiar with this from having played *The End Game,* page 24.)

Ask students to identify things in their ideal life that are a means to some further end. To do this they should ask 'Why do I want this? What will I gain from it?' For example, 'being taller' (in category 2) may be a means to playing volleyball, but what is playing volleyball a means to – health, success, friendships, an even suntan?

Eventually students should have a list of values or goals, and should be able to give a reason for everything in their ideal life.

Stage Three – In this last stage students should try to reduce the things they want, their ends, to as few as possible.

In pairs, students should take their lists of ends and ask whether they have broader, more abstract reasons for their choices, for example: happiness, pleasure, contentment, respect, love, success, health.

During feedback on the final stage, ask the class whether everyone's values can be reduced to a few, or perhaps just one ultimate value?

Hints and tips

■ Make sure that students are familiar with the distinction between means and ends before they embark on Stage Two.

■ You might want to stop at Stage One. An enjoyable alternative enables members of the class to share their ideal life with one another to lead to an *Optimum Life* – sharing ideals that everyone in the class agrees with. Once students have contributed one or two of their ideals to the grid on the board, invite students to vote which items should be scrubbed off the board – if three or four students vote against an item, then it's wiped off. What remains is a 'lowest common denominator' ideal life.

■ Point out that 'Environment' does not just mean the weather, but the world around us in the broadest sense.

Points for discussion

■ The main issue for students to think about is *why* they have written what they have on the grid – what will those things help them achieve?

■ Encourage students to ask whether there are many ends or just a few, or perhaps just a single ultimate end that we can reduce all other ends to.

■ Does the whole class agree on the goals of life? Some students might take a HEDONISTIC position, claiming that the ultimate goal of all actions is pleasure, and that everything we do is aimed at getting as much pleasure as possible. Other students may find that they agree with CHARLES DARWIN or RICHARD DAWKINS, that our purpose is determined by a million years of evolution, and is simply to survive, reproduce and take care of our offspring until they reproduce. Other students may take Aristotle's line and argue that our aim is to flourish and fulfil our potential in order to achieve EUDAIMONIA.

■ Many students might claim that the only thing any of us really want is pleasure. Philosophers who hold this view are called 'psychological hedonists'. Is hedonism even meaningful? You could ask students to think about the following issues:

— Would anyone substitute a life of pure pleasure for this life? Ask students if they would plug themselves into a pleasure machine, or be locked into a 'pleasure cupboard' for the rest of their lives.

— We may question whether pleasure is a distinct QUALIA at all. Take as an example drinking a cup of tea: is it possible to separate the distinct sensation of pleasure from the sensation of its taste, its warmth, its milky sweetness, its caffeine content? Aristotle would say that pleasure wasn't a distinct sensation at all, rather it 'perfects the activity'. In other words, it's a kind of heightened awareness, but not a sensation that can be separated from the activity.

— Many of our actions aim at avoiding pain – and this is not at all identical with pleasure. So perhaps there are at least two goals in life: pursuit of happiness and avoidance of pain.

— If humans always aim to maximise pleasure, then why do we ever act selflessly, for other people? Is it just because it makes us feel good? Furthermore, why do people sacrifice their lives or their happiness for others?

TEACHER'S PAGE

4 The M.O.R.A.L. Questionnaire

About the game

A questionnaire designed to explore students' moral intuitions. No previous knowledge of ethics is required, and the exercise is an excellent way of introducing the concept of morality to a class.

General information

Length of time:	30–45 minutes (15 minutes questionnaire, 20–30 minutes feedback)
Group / Class size:	Works best in pairs, but can be used as an individual or small group task. Class size unlimited.
Materials required:	Photocopies of *The M.O.R.A.L. Questionnaire*

Aims

To investigate the difference between actions / situations that we intuitively think of as 'moral' and actions / situations that we think of as 'morally neutral'.

How to play

1 Ask students to complete *The M.O.R.A.L. Questionnaire* in pairs and to write down their reasons for making each decision.
2 You should then lead a feedback session on each example, attempting to draw out the reasons why some actions are morally neutral, and why others are not. (See the table on the next page.)

Hints and tips

■ Question students in detail on the reasons they give.

■ It is useful to focus on the morally neutral actions as these will help the class determine what makes an action a moral one (i.e. good or bad). For example, if an action does not involve humans then is it always morally neutral? (Can it involve some other suitable moral agent such as an alien, God, or a sophisticated robot?)

■ Students may try to be inventive and awkward, and may claim that each scenario could be good or bad by making up some extra information. For example, take Situation 8 'You complete 15 passes in a 1–1 draw at a local hockey match.' Normally considered neutral, this could be considered a morally good act if twenty school children were tied to one of the goal posts ready to be killed unless 15 successful passes were completed. Tell students to take each scenario as it is written.

■ Emphasise to the class that what they are judging is not whether a particular action is good or bad. The exercise is designed to bring out an even more fundamental distinction, between morally neutral and morally significant actions. It is interesting and enjoyable for students to discuss the pros and cons of killing ants, but you should be looking for the reasons why students say a particular act is morally significant.

■ As students make suggestions it is helpful to write down on the board the reasons why an action is morally neutral or good / bad. You will probably end up with two columns looking something like this:

Moral actions	Morally neutral actions

An action is moral if it:
 • involves humans / moral agents
 • is intended
 • affects others
     in a harmful way
     in a beneficial way
	An action is morally neutral if it:
	 • involves animals / nature
	 • is accidental
	 • does not affect others at all
	 • does not affect others
	     in a harmful / beneficial way

Points for discussion

■ **Situations 1, 2, 4 and 5** In what way do humans differ from animals or from 'natural acts'? Does this include all humans all the time? Many philosophers would say that humans are different morally from animals only insofar as they are capable of freely and thoughtfully chosen actions – they are 'moral agents'. Any creature that can freely and thoughtfully choose its actions will count as a moral agent, perhaps even some aliens. The question is what counts as a 'free' and 'thoughtful' choice. (See *The Thing from Planet Z* on page 36 for another activity on moral agency.)

■ **Situation 1** What difference does it make to our judgements if God exists? Some atheists, such as John Stuart Mill, have argued that if God is the almighty creator of the universe then natural disasters such as earthquakes, droughts and diseases are all the result of a moral agent, and are therefore moral acts. This debate is known as the PROBLEM OF EVIL.

■ **Situations 3, 6, 10, 11, 12 and 13** How important is intention? Some philosophers argue that it is not the motive but the consequences of an action that make it moral. If an action was done with evil intent but had no effect on anyone, would we then count it as a moral act? (See *Universalisability Challenge* on page 65 for an activity that introduces Kant's theory of intention in ethics.)

■ **Situations 4, 5, 6 and 7** What is meant by 'affecting others'? We may decide that a moral act is one that affects others, but there is still a huge amount of ambiguity about the word 'others'. Some thinkers argue that 'others' should include mammals, or insects, or plant life, or the world as a whole. Those things that are on the receiving end of a moral action are known as moral patients. In the exercise you might discuss whether killing ants (or bacteria or amoeba) is different from killing rabbits, and if so, why. You may want to suggest that 'others' could even include your future self. In which case, even though you are in outer space and will never meet anyone else, you can still commit an immoral act by taking up smoking – you are harming your future self. (See *Drawing the Line* on page 44 for further investigations of moral patienthood.)

■ **Situations 8** This is morally neutral, though see the comment on this matter under *Hints and tips.*

■ **Situations 9, 10, 11, 12 and 13** What is meant by 'harm' or 'benefit'? This is another huge area of debate, especially as utilitarians claim that an action is only moral insofar as it produces harm or benefits. If this is the case, then they must be able to define these terms if they are to have a tenable theory. Harm may be physical, emotional or psychological, and it might also include depriving others of happiness. Benefits may also be physical or psychological. They may be positive, in that they produce happiness; or negative, in that they prevent pain or harm. (See *Health or Wealth?* on page 70 for further problems with utilitarianism.)

STUDENT'S PAGE

The M.O.R.A.L. Questionnaire

The Government welcomes you to the Ministry of Righteous Action in Life (M.O.R.A.L.). As you know, this department has been set up to look into the moral affairs of the nation. A select committee of the Righteous and the Repugnant has been chosen for their expertise in right and wrong acts.

As members of this committee, your brief is to establish the Moral Agenda for the Millennium by dividing up all actions into the Good, the Bad and the Neutral. Tick one box after each example: A if it is a good act, B if it is a bad act, or C if it is morally neutral.

1 A tree falls in a forest and crushes a cute deer.   A ☐ B ☐ C ☐

2 A killer whale toys with a seal it has half-killed – batting it into the air with its tail and catching it with its teeth. It takes twenty minutes for the seal to die. The whale leaves it to rot on the ocean floor.   A ☐ B ☐ C ☐

3 You deliberately step on someone's toe in a lift but pretend it was an accident.   A ☐ B ☐ C ☐

4 You accidentally poison your neighbour's dog.   A ☐ B ☐ C ☐

5 You beat your friend in an ant-killing competition (with a winning combination of bleach and boiling water).   A ☐ B ☐ C ☐

6 When you were at school, you persistently bullied a classmate.   A ☐ B ☐ C ☐

7 A billionaire builds herself a space rocket and leaves Earth for ever. For the rest of her life none of her actions ever affect another living thing. Could any of her future actions be good or bad (A) or will they all be morally neutral (B)?   A ☐ B ☐

8 You complete 15 passes in a 1–1 draw at a local hockey match.   A ☐ B ☐ C ☐

9 An orphanage is set up to help the victims of a war in an African state.   A ☐ B ☐ C ☐

10 A builder shouts 'Nice legs!' to a person walking past.   A ☐ B ☐ C ☐

11 You stop to help a blind man cross the road but fail to notice the oncoming, unstoppable juggernaut that injures you both.   A ☐ B ☐ C ☐

12 An evil scientist releases a new biochemical into the water supply of a large city intending to kill millions of people. However, this chemical, when diluted, turns out to be a harmless cure for cancer and countless lives are saved.   A ☐ B ☐ C ☐

5 The Thing from Planet Z

About the game

A discussion exercise that raises the question 'What makes humans so special when it comes to ethics?'

General information

Length of time: 40–50 minutes (20 minutes for the exercise, 20–30 minutes for feedback)

Group / Class size: Groups of 4–6, class size 6–30

Materials required: One copy of the three worksheets per group

---

Aims

This activity is designed to encourage discussion of two issues:
1 The difficulty of defining human beings in any ethically useful way.
2 The concept of NECESSARY AND SUFFICIENT CONDITIONS.

How to play

1 Divide the class into groups. Each team represents the crew of a spaceship on a mission to discover extra-terrestrial life. Each group should decide upon a name for their team.

2 The aim of the game is for teams to arrive at a method of assessing whether an alien should be treated as a person, and thus be given 'human rights'.

3 There are two stages to the game, and for each stage there is a worksheet for students to fill in.

4 **Stage One** – Give out Student's pages 1 and 2 of *The Thing from Planet Z*. Page 1 outlines the situation that students find themselves in and the aim of their mission. *Phase 1* (on page 2) is their first task: to brainstorm ways of determining whether a particular life form is human-like or not. Is the alien a person? During this brainstorm, students should be thinking about what features make us different from other things – so different, in fact, that most people think that humans have a higher moral status than other things. If the alien shares these features with us then it too should be respected as a person.
Students might want to think about:
■ How intelligent / emotional / aware is the alien?
■ Is it conscious or even self-conscious?
■ Does it move / act / behave in a complex way?
■ Does it have a mental representation of the world?
■ Does it have beliefs and desires?
■ Is it creative?
Students must think about how they could check or verify any of these questions.

5   Students should write down the questions about the features they think are important in the *first* column of the *Phase 1* sheet, e.g. 'Can it feel pain?' The other two columns should be ignored at this stage.

6   **Stage Two** – give out the *Phase 2* sheet. Now comes the difficult part. Students need to scrutinise the features they have chosen, and test them to see whether they really are fundamental in establishing whether a creature is a person, and is owed special moral treatment.

7   Students should take each feature in turn. They should apply the first test to the feature: can they think of a person / human that does not have this feature? If so, they should write it in the second column and they should also think twice about including this feature amongst their final three choices. This first test tells us whether a particular feature is a necessary condition of being a person (or a human).

8   Students should then apply the second test: can they think of any non-human / non-person that has this feature? If so, they should write their example in the third column, and they should think twice about including this feature in their final choices. This second test tells us whether a particular feature is a sufficient condition of being a person / human.

9   **Stage Three** – Finally, students should choose those three features that best define or identify a creature as a person. United Nations Mission Control (UNMC), i.e. you, will judge the utility of the features and declare a winner.

Hints and tips

■   Read the *Philosophical background* at the end of this activity for details on the distinction between necessary and sufficient conditions.

■   Groups might need 20 minutes or so and some help, depending on their familiarity with this kind of task. The competitive element will need to be carefully balanced with judgements about the quality of the end product. Send back UNMC forms if they are not up to scratch, and warn groups not to sacrifice quality for speed.

■   Some more sample questions if groups are stuck:

Does it ever worry about things or get depressed?
Does it understand the concept of death?
Does it have art / literature / creativity?
Is it self-conscious?
Can it communicate?
How sophisticated is its representation of the world?

■   It is possible that some groups, even after 20 minutes, will have no definitive answers. Whatever the outcome, discussing the questions and subjecting them to analysis and selection should be fruitful.

Points for discussion

■ The first point of this exercise is for students to think about what makes something a moral agent or a person. What features must a creature have in order for us to elevate it to the status of 'person', something worthy of rights?

■ One way that students could look at the issue of 'right-worthiness' is by considering what they would have to do to persuade an alien that they deserved moral rights. How could an alien, who presumably would be just as mystified as us by the encounter, tell whether we were persons?

■ The second point of this exercise is for students to think about whether it is possible to define a 'person' by coming up with necessary and sufficient conditions for it. This is very, very difficult, especially for a vague concept like a 'person'. To define a human being is easier, but the problem is that we are then picking out morally irrelevant features like 'DNA type' – or perhaps all there is to being a person is having human DNA.

■ How easy is it actually to define 'human being'? Definitions of 'human being' sometimes seem to exclude infants or people on life-support machines, or to include animals such as the higher primates (does this matter?), or they focus on physical attributes like 'number of chromosomes' which seem ethically meaningless.

■ If the features students have picked out are too general (e.g. 'Is it intelligent?') then it is possible that the alien is simply a computer or a robot of some kind, in which case shouldn't it be treated like one? Or it could be an animal, or a very young or very stupid human-like creature. How should it be treated in these cases?

■ Why do people treat humans in a morally different way from other species? This question is fundamental to any discussion of animal rights and it is hard to say why, in particular, humans should have any special moral privileges. If we are going to draw ethical boundaries between species, what are our grounds for doing so? Do any of the criteria that students have listed carry with them a moral licence of some kind? For some philosophers the fact that an organism is conscious, or can feel pain, is enough for it to be treated with the same respect as a human being. (This issue is raised specifically in *Drawing the Line*, page 44.)

■ Can any of the criteria be replicated in non-organic or mechanical creatures? (The film *Bladerunner* raises this aspect of A.I. in a fascinating way.) Imagine that we could develop computers that become as intelligent as humans, that speak and act in ways very similar to us. Should we then search for some further criteria that retains our special moral status, and distinguishes us from computers, such as 'warm-blooded' or 'free'? Or should we start treating them as 'honorary humans'? (perhaps as a result of pressure from the 'Computer Rights' movement!)

Philosophical background

This exercise can be used to explore the difficulties of finding the exact definition of a concept. There may be several qualities that form the definition of something; philosophers use the notion of necessary and sufficient conditions as a way of expressing those defining properties. To make this clearer we should look at an example of something that is easily defined: a triangle. We want to know the necessary and sufficient conditions of a triangle, in other words the properties that a shape must have if it is to count as a triangle.

Let us take the idea of a *necessary condition*. If we think about every triangle then we realise that every triangle has three sides. So the shape that we call 'triangle' must possess the property of 'having three sides' if it is to count as a triangle. One way of testing this is to think about whether there are any examples of triangles that don't have three sides (that is the point of the second column in *Phase 1*). Of course there are no examples of triangles that don't have three sides: in other words 'having three sides' is a *necessary* part of being a triangle. We can express the idea of a necessary condition by saying:

> *Only if* something has three sides *then* it is a triangle.

The second column of *Phase 1* tests whether a property is a necessary condition of being a human. Is 'consciousness' a necessary property of being human? One might have thought so, but what then of people who have been knocked out, or are asleep or in a coma – have they ceased to be human? Perhaps a better way of expressing this property is to say 'having a propensity to be conscious'. Is this refined criterion a necessary condition? Well, as we saw above, we just need to think of humans that don't possess this quality and if we can't think of any then yes, the propensity to be conscious is a necessary condition of being human.

We have seen that it is one of the properties of a triangle that it has three sides, but is 'having three sides' enough to fully define a triangle? One way to think about this is to think of other things that have three sides but are not triangles:

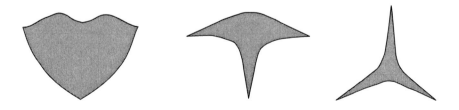

So, the quality of 'having three sides' is not enough to define a shape as a triangle, we need further conditions. Let us now look at the concept of *sufficient condition*.

By continuing with the triangle example we can refine our criterion to make it into a sufficient condition: 'having three *straight* sides'. We can test this by thinking about whether there are any examples of non-triangles that have three straight sides. There aren't any such examples and we can conclude that if a shape is known to have three straight sides then that is enough for us to guarantee that it is a triangle. We can express the idea of a sufficient condition by saying:

> *If* a shape has three straight sides *then* it is a triangle.

That is the point of the third column in *Phase 1*. Take one of the criteria that the students have brainstormed, for example 'having a propensity to be conscious'. Now if it is possible to think of a non-human that also possesses that particular quality (dogs perhaps), then possessing that quality by itself is not enough to define something as 'human' (in philosophical terms it is not *sufficient*). Some psychologists and philosophers have thought that 'self-consciousness' was a sufficient condition of being human, because they claimed that other animals were not self-conscious. However, this is debatable (given the response that dolphins, pygmy chimps, etc. have to their reflection in a mirror).

In logical terms, the defining properties are those that are both *necessary* and *sufficient*, and this is expressed by combining the 'if' and the 'only if':

> *If and only if* a shape has three straight sides *then* it is a triangle.

The Thing from Planet Z

Mission not impossible but quite difficult ...

Eighteen months ago and a million light years away, you and your crew members set out on a mission: to find intelligent life in another galaxy. Recent reports from United Nations Mission Control (UNMC) suggest that an extra-terrestrial being has been discovered on Planet Z.

The company that employs you, SolarTech, have taken no chances and have sent several other crews on the same mission. Your jobs are in jeopardy as rival spacecraft close in on Planet Z. Who is going to be first to make contact and secure the new life form for SolarTech to use? It's all down to you now.

UNMC have formally requested that each crew must send back a report on the nature of the life form. You have to establish whether this alien is sufficiently human-like for it to be treated in the same way as a person.

If the alien turns out merely to be a kind of cosmic vegetable, then SolarTech have permission to eat it, grow it and experiment on it as they wish. If, however, it is as complex as a person, then SolarTech, and everyone else, must respect its life and autonomy. In other words, it is down to you and your team to work out what place this alien has in our moral system.

Your mission *You must decide upon three features that can be used to identify whether the alien should be counted as a person. These three features will be transmitted back to UNMC and the first team to get three useful questions back to Mission Control will be handsomely rewarded by SolarTech.*

STUDENT'S PAGE

Phase 1: Brainstorm

How can we tell whether this thing we have found is like us? What sort of features should we be looking for? Crew members should think of as many features as possible, e.g. Can it communicate? Take it in turns to think of features – go for quantity at this stage, don't criticise or try to select. Write the questions in the first column on your sheet, and ignore the other two columns for the moment.

Starting suggestions

- *Is it intelligent?* This question is too vague – how can we tell whether something is intelligent?
- *Can it feel pain?* Again this needs to be made more specific – how can we tell whether something feels pain?

QUESTIONS	Can you think of a human that does not have this feature?	Can you think of a non-human that does have this feature?
Is it intelligent? Can it feel pain?		

Phase 2: Select three features

Now your task is to select those three features that you think best identify something as a person. Go through each of the questions you have written down and test whether they are really useful questions.

For each question ask:

1 Can you think of examples of human beings who lack this quality or attribute? If so, write down these examples in the second column of the Phase 1 sheet.
2 Can you think of examples of non-humans that have this quality or attribute? Write them down in the third column of the Phase 1 sheet.

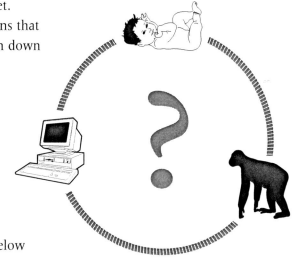

The winning questions will be those that pick out some feature or quality that all humans have and only humans have. But finding such a quality might be impossible, so go for the best questions you can.

When you have finished, fill out the form below for transmission to UNMC.

UNMC investigation into life on Planet Z

We, the undersigned, would investigate the following questions in order to judge whether the life form on Planet Z is sufficiently 'human' to be accorded human rights.

a ....

b ....

c ....

Signed: ....

The crew of Spaceship ....

Exploring Ethics © JOHN MURRAY

6 Drawing the Line

About the game

An exercise that asks the question 'Where do we draw the line when it comes to harming animals?'

General information

Length of time:	20–25 minutes (15 minutes for the exercise, 10 minutes for feedback)
Group / class size:	Group size 1–3, class size unlimited
Materials required:	A worksheet for each student

Aims

To introduce students to the concept of a moral patient and to invite students to question the consistency of their own intuitions about what people should and should not harm.

How to play

1 Give out the worksheets.
2 Students should fill in each row by shading ▨ or putting a cross ☒ in the box if they think it is morally wrong to do a certain act to a certain creature. If they think an act is morally permissible or neutral, they should leave the square blank.
3 If a student thinks that it depends on the situation, then they should write 'it depends' in the box, but be prepared to justify their decision later.
4 When students have finished filling in the boxes they should then discuss in pairs whether any pattern has emerged, and whether there are any reasons for this pattern.

Hints and tips

■ In the first row, students should understand that 'it' refers to themselves.
■ To help students with the second part of the exercise you should ask students to see whether there is any relationship between the amount of pain inflicted and the type of creature it is being inflicted upon.
■ Examples of patterns might be:
The less like a human it is, the more permissible it is to inflict pain without good reason.
It is permissible to inflict pain on anything that is not self-aware.
It is not permissible to willingly inflict pain on anything unless you have a good reason.

TEACHER'S PAGE

■ Ask students to pick out any anomalies to their rule / pattern, and to give a reason for these exceptions. For example, they might think it permissible to abort fetuses, but not to kill children if they interfere with their quality of life, but can they explain why abortion, but not infanticide, is morally permissible?

■ You should feel free to introduce or add to their examples, e.g. a human in a coma; a human who lacks any AUTONOMY or agency (for example, someone who is severely brain-damaged); an alien (this ties in with *The Thing From Planet Z*); an incredibly sophisticated computer such as HAL in *2001: A Space Odyssey*; or a favourite pet.

Points for discussion

■ A moral patient is anything that can be the recipient of a moral action but opinions vary widely as to how far the concept of 'moral patient' extends. Most people would agree that stones and other inanimate natural objects are not moral patients – we can do anything to them without doing anything that is morally wrong. But, are plants, insects or other animals moral patients? The question is: where do we draw the line? What features are we looking for in deciding whether something is a moral patient?

■ There are lots of questions you can ask students at the end of the exercise. Did they find a pattern? If they didn't, why didn't they? Is it simply arbitrary what we can and can't inflict pain on? If they did, is there any reason for this pattern? Is what counts as a moral patient based simply on individual tastes and preferences (although this seems an appalling conclusion to come to)? Are there any anomalies? Are there any reasons for these anomalies?

■ What is striking about this exercise is how varied and random students' responses are. Some students will base their decision on how rare / common a creature is, others on how like a grown human being it is, others on how cuddly it is. (Is cuddliness a genuinely good criterion for not harming a creature?)

■ Another feature that may strike you is the propensity for students to value humans above all else. Many philosophers, PETER SINGER amongst them, have seen this as SPECIESISM, a form of prejudice akin to racism or sexism. You should ask students whether there are any good reasons for giving humans privileges above other creatures. JEREMY BENTHAM said that what is important is not whether a creature can think, but whether it can feel pain.

■ This exercise may bring out the incoherence and inconsistency of our ordinary moral beliefs. You may see that it is incredibly common, and incredibly worrying, for students to be unable to give any convincing reasons why it is morally permissible to harm one creature, but not another.

Drawing the Line

Shade / put a cross in the box if it is always or mostly wrong to do this to these →	Make life-changing decisions on its behalf	Kill / destroy it because it interferes with your quality of life	Own it, or deprive it of its freedom without any reason	Kill / destroy it in order to eat or use parts of it	Perform harmful experiments on it	Harm it for your own pleasure	Kill / destroy it without any reason
Yourself							
Another human adult							
A child							
A 16-week-old fetus							
A chimp							
A whale							
A rabbit							
An ant							
A plant							
A beach							

7 Moral Dilemmas

About the game

Students must make moral judgements, supported by reasons, for a range of tricky situations.

General information

Length of time: Any length depending on the number of questions discussed

Group / Class size: Groups of 2–6, class size unlimited

Materials required: Photocopies of the *Moral Dilemmas* worksheets

---

Aims

To encourage students to make reasoned ethical judgements and to enable students to apply previous learning about moral theories to concrete examples.

How to play

The dilemmas could be used in a number of ways; here are two suggestions:

1 Split the class into groups and ask each group to arrive at a resolution to each dilemma. During feedback the groups must then justify their answers.

2 Split the class into different groups and ask each group to solve the dilemma from a different ethical perspective. For example, one group could be broadly Christian, another group utilitarian, another Kantian, another can make judgements according to the 'moral majority' as might be represented in a tabloid newspaper. The purpose of the latter group is to explore the way some newspapers use hyperbole and hysteria to generate immediate and reactionary judgements – this is the opposite of a reasoned critical / philosophical judgement. The rest of the class has to decide whether the group correctly solved the dilemma in accordance with the ethical perspective of the group they represent. Other ideas for groups might be: Muslim, Buddhist, Aristotelian, anarchist, humanist or existentialist. See *Points for discussion* for suggested answers.

Hints and tips

■ Essentially, these situations are stimuli for group discussion, with potential for feedback to the whole class. If you want a quiet lesson rather than group work, you can give students the questions to think about individually – but you should still be prepared for discussion after thinking time.

■ The situations are deliberately exaggerated and highly unlikely – students shouldn't get too bogged down in extraneous detail (though some details may be ethically relevant).

Points for discussion

Note We have provided some possible answers, but these should in no way be taken to be the actual views of Christians, Kantians, etc.

■ **Situation 1** is a classic test of utilitarian values: *are four lives worth more than one life?* If so, can utilitarianism justify taking one life to save four? It also raises the issue of voluntary euthanasia: should we respect someone's AUTONOMY to the extent that we allow them to take their own lives, even if it is to help others? Would students' answers change if the young man had been suffering from a terminal illness himself or if he wanted to commit suicide? SLIPPERY SLOPE arguments are often invoked here: if we allow voluntary euthanasia to occur, then where will the killing end?

A Christian view	No,	only God has the right to give and take lives, with certain exceptions such as a just war.
A Kantian view	No,	every life should be treated as an end in itself, and not as a means to saving other lives.
A utilitarian view	Yes,	a classical utilitarian would say it maximises happiness.
The Daily Tabloid	**No:**	*'Four Transplants and a Funeral – Stop This Doctor of Death!'*

■ **Situation 2** raises difficulties with absolutist and DEONTOLOGICAL rules and obligations: *what value will promise-making have if promises are easily broken?* Do we have obligations to the dead? How would we feel if we knew that our dying wishes would not be honoured?

A Christian view	Yes,	we should respect our family's wishes, especially our parents'.
A Kantian view	Yes,	if we didn't keep promises then they wouldn't exist, so we have a duty to keep them.
A utilitarian view	No,	for an act utilitarian the money might be better given to a charity, or anything that maximises happiness.
	Yes,	for a rule utilitarian it would be better if everyone did keep their promises – everyone would be happier.
The Daily Tabloid	**Yes:**	*'Hallowed be Thy Turf'*

■ **Situation 3** raises the ACTS AND OMISSIONS distinction – *is there a moral difference between killing someone and letting someone die?* In this case the consequences are roughly the same – only one person is going to die. The ACT UTILITARIAN might think differently, choosing to weigh up the relative values of the lives of the baby or the tramp. The RULE UTILITARIAN might consider the consequences of following the rule 'occasionally it's morally permissible to kill people'.

A Christian view	No,	to alter the points would be to actively kill someone; to leave them on this occasion is to let God's plan run its natural course.

A Kantian view	No,	we have a duty not to kill anyone, so omitting to act is the better of two evils.
A utiliarian view	Yes,	for a utilitarian the life of the baby might be considered to be more valuable because of its potential future happiness. The tramp on the other hand is perceived to have little utility to society.
The Daily Tabloid	**Yes:**	*'LOCO HERO! Trainspotter makes Brave Baby-Saving Decision'*

■ **Situation 4** also raises the acts / omissions distinction, but in a more extreme form: *which is worse: causing a large amount of harm by omitting to act, or causing a smaller amount of harm through active involvement?* It also raises the question of whether the aims of an action justify the method by which they were achieved (see also 5 below). There may be a further issue: if we do kill the prisoner, then what effect will it have on the rest of our life?

A Christian view	No,	human life is sacred and killing is against God's moral law.
A Kantian view	No,	we have a duty not to kill, we can never universalise the rule 'kill'.
A utilitarian view	Yes,	for a classical utilitarian we should kill a prisoner, thus maximising happiness.
The Daily Tabloid	**No**	*or else: 'Sick Brit Brings Shame on Our Nation'*

■ **Situation 5** raises several questions, in particular *do the ends justify the means?* Should justice, or equality, or utility be achieved by whatever means necessary? What would be the consequences of encouraging Robin Hood-type thieves to redistribute wealth by their own methods? A further issue is one of acts and omissions – do we have a duty as citizens to report crimes, or should we not get involved?

A Christian view	Yes,	stealing is against God's moral law.
A Kantian view	Yes,	we have a duty to respect property.
A utilitarian view	No,	for an act utilitarian it might best maximise happiness if the money is given to those truly in need.
	Yes,	for a rule utilitarian society is generally happier if we respect rules about property and ownership.
The Daily Tabloid	**Yes:**	*'ROBBING HOODS – Upright Citizen Foils Evil Plan by Relief Workers'*

■ **Situation 6** (as in Situation 2) is about promise-keeping. *Do we have a duty, or does it maximise utility, to keep ridiculous promises?*

A Christian view	Yes,	once we have made a promise to someone we should respect it.
A Kantian view	Yes,	we have a duty to keep promises (if everyone broke promises then no one would make them).
A utilitarian view	No,	it would be absurd to destroy the garden and waste all that beer, which could be donated to a local charity for a raffle.
The Daily Tabloid	No:	*'DON'T BE-ER FOOL: DRINKS ON THE HOUSE, NOT ON THE GARDEN!'*

■ **In Situation 7** you have to choose between various evils, and it is an exaggerated version of many moral dilemmas. *Is it better to do nothing?* This raises the acts / omissions distinction again. If we have to make a decision, how do we place a value on the various lives that are at stake?

A Christian view	(d)	Only God can give life, and only God can take it away. This isn't one of the exceptions to the command: do not kill.
A Kantian view		Possibly (d). This dilemma brings out a major problem with deontological ethics – how do we decide between conflicting rules?
A utilitarian view	(a)	It's a horrible choice to make, but it depends whether you think minimising pain (save the researchers) is more important than maximising happiness (save the comedians). You may go for a 'head count', but do unborn babies count as person / moral patients?
The Daily Tabloid	(a)	*'BATTING ON A STICKY WICKET – Cricket Ace saves Pregnant Lovelies and Cancer Boffins'*

■ **Situation 8** is about telling the truth – *should we always tell the truth*, as deontological theories would dictate? Again the utilitarian may disagree.

A Christian view	Yes,	we should always tell the truth.
A Kantian view	Yes,	it is our duty to tell the truth (we cannot universalise lying).
A utilitarian view	No,	for an act utilitarian it might maximise happiness if you didn't tell him, but instead talked about quorn or tofu.
	Yes,	for a rule utilitarian it might best maximise happiness if everyone told the truth – that way trust is maintained.
The Daily Tabloid	No:	*'Vegan Nut-ter in Teatime Tantrum!'*

■ **Situation 9** is a practical ethical problem – *is it better to divide resources and share equally, or for some people to have more than others?* The former sounds fine, but what if it leads to everyone suffering or dying, when in the latter case, at least one person might be happier or survive?

A Christian view   No,   God created us all equal, and the chocolate should be distributed equally.

A Kantian view   No,   we should act from duty, not from desire, and here it is clearly our duty, as leader of the expedition, to ensure that everyone is helped.

A utilitarian view   Yes,   it is better that at least one person survives than everyone else dies.

The Daily Tabloid   **No:**   *'Marathon Expedition Flakes Out as Selfish Survivor Scoffs the Lot!'*

Moral Dilemmas

Give reasons for your opinions and try to consider all the implications of your decisions. If your answers tend to be 'It depends', discuss what they depend on and why.

1 You are a doctor working in a hospital. One day a healthy young man walks into reception and says that several members of his family are in danger of dying because they need organ transplants. One needs a heart, one needs a lung, two need kidneys and one needs a liver. He wants you to give him a painless but lethal injection, then take his organs and use them to save his relatives. If you don't he says that he will go to a back-street doctor who has agreed to 'have a go' at the operations for a small price.

   Should you allow this youth to sacrifice his life in order to save his family?

2 On his deathbed your father asks you to promise him that when he dies you will spread his ashes over the hallowed ground of Old Stratford, Ladchester City's football stadium. He has been a life-long supporter and you know how much it means to him so you promise you will. He dies a happy man and leaves you £10,000 in his will. You make some enquiries with the football club and Ladchester City agree to let you carry out your father's wish, but they explain that they charge £10,000 for this service.

   Do you keep your promise?

3 An empty train is fast approaching a junction. You are standing by the points. If you do nothing, the train will go straight on and will run over a baby who has crawled onto the line. If you alter the points, the train will be diverted and will run over a drunken old tramp who is lying on the track.

   Do you divert the train?

STUDENT'S PAGE

4   You are on a business trip visiting a foreign country and, as part of your tour, your hosts show you round a local prison. You are shocked to find that the guards are about to execute six political prisoners. The prison governor explains that as today is a festival, you have the opportunity to save the lives of five of these prisoners: in a gesture of goodwill to his important guest he explains that if you will shoot one of the prisoners, then the others will be spared.

Do you kill one of the prisoners yourself?

5   You pick up the telephone to make a call but the line is crossed and you overhear a conversation between two charity workers. From their conversation you gather that they have decided to break the law in a last ditch effort to raise funds. They are planning an armed robbery on a large bank and will anonymously distribute the cash to a variety of charities.

Do you call the police?

6   Your neighbour wins a lifetime's supply (about 10,000 cans) of your favourite beer in a crossword competition. As he is a teetotaller, he starts to use the beer (10 cans a day) to 'water' his garden, believing it will nourish his plants. You know that this is complete nonsense and will in fact damage the plants. One day he calls round saying that he is going on holiday for two months. He asks if you would keep watering his plants with the 600 cans of beer he leaves you. You promise faithfully that you will, but what do you do when he goes?

Do you keep your promise?

Exploring Ethics © JOHN MURRAY

STUDENT'S PAGE

7 A fiendish madman has kidnapped a group of people including yourself and taken you to a large disused barn. Alongside one wall of the barn are crates of explosives. You are a world-famous cricketer and the kidnapper fastens one of your legs to a stake in front of the explosives. To your right he binds up a group of four popular comedians; to your left he ties up four women at various stages of pregnancy; and straight ahead of you he chains four of the world's leading researchers into AIDS and cancer. Everyone is gagged. In front of you is an automatic bowling machine. Before leaving, the kidnapper hands you a cricket bat and tells you 'In half an hour the bowling machine will deliver a ball – the ball contains a grenade. If you do not hit the ball it will strike the explosives behind you and everyone will die. You must decide where to hit the ball – and thus who is saved and who is killed.'

There are only four possible choices. Do you:
a hit the ball to the right, killing the comedians?
b hit the ball to the left, killing the mothers-to-be?
c hit the ball straight, killing the scientists?
d leave the grenade to hit the explosives thus killing everyone?

8 At a local barbecue, your vegan neighbour takes a big bowlful of your pork, bean and bacon hot-pot. Not knowing what it is, she really enjoys it: 'The best food I have had since I was in New York – can I have the recipe?' She is already half way through her bowl.

Do you stop her and tell her what she is eating?

9 Thick fog descends on the scouts expedition that you are leading. It forces you to set up camp and just as well, because a blizzard starts an hour later. After two days in the storm, with no immediate prospect of rescue, your food runs out. Four hours later, you discover a small slab of milk chocolate. Divided between eight, the chocolate pieces would be minuscule, and you are the hungriest person there.

Do you eat the chocolate yourself?

8 Are You a Humanist?

About the game

A questionnaire designed to help students consider the relationship of religious / spiritual beliefs to morality.

General information

Length of time: 15 minutes for questionnaire, 15–30 for discussion
Group / Class size: Students work individually, class size unlimited
Materials required: Photocopies of the *Are You a Humanist?* questionnaire and answer sheets

Aims

To allow students to examine their personal beliefs and the effects these may have on their values.

How to play

1 Students simply fill in the multiple-choice questionnaire.
2 After 10 minutes or so, hand out the answer sheet so that the class can work out their individual scores.
3 Give feedback on the students' choices and their scores.

Hints and tips

When students count up the symbols they may find that they have an equal number of both ☺ and H. Humanists and believers do share the same beliefs about many issues, this is reflected in the fact that some answers may score both a humanist symbol and a believer symbol. Students should count both in their scores. Ask them to decide which camp they think they fall into, and what their decision is based on.

Points for discussion

A good place to begin might be with questions that were found challenging or difficult or where the answer was not as expected. Points that may come up:

■ Is there a connection between religious faith and morality?
■ What is humanism?
■ Can you have religious faith and still be a humanist?
■ How difficult is it for an atheist to make moral judgements?
■ Must all atheists believe that morality is subjective or relative?

Are You a Humanist?

Tick the statements that are closest to your point of view.

1 Does God exist?
a I am sure there is a God ruling over the universe.
b I don't know.
c There is no evidence that any god exists, so I'll assume that there isn't one.
d It depends what you mean by God, but I think so.

2 When I die ...
a I will be rewarded in Heaven if I am good and punished in Hell if I am bad.
b That will be the end of me.
c I will live on in people's memories or the work I have done or through my children.
d I will survive in some kind of afterlife.

3 How did the Universe begin?
a It was set up as an experiment by extremely intelligent aliens from another universe.
b I don't know.
c The scientific explanations are the best ones available – no gods were involved.
d God created it.

4 The theory that life on Earth evolved gradually over billions of years is ...
a True, there is plenty of evidence from fossils showing
that this is how it happened.
b Likely to be true, but I think God had a part in it too.
c Probably true, because my science teacher says it's true.
d Just a theory. My religion tells the true story.

5 When I am in trouble or feeling unhappy what works best for me is ...
a Help and advice from friends and family.
b Getting on with life – I usually manage to sort things out.
c Talking to my doctor.
d Prayer.

6 When I look at a beautiful view I think that ...
a It must have been designed by God.
b This is what life is all about – I feel good.
c It would be a nice place for a motorway.
d We ought to do everything possible to protect this
for future generations.

STUDENT'S PAGE

7 I can tell right from wrong by ...
a Reading a holy book or listening to a religious leader.
b Accepting what my parents and teachers say.
c Thinking hard about the probable consequences of actions and their effects on other people.
d I don't really think about it much – people should just do as they like.

8 About good and evil, I think ...
a There is evil in the world and God exists to help us overcome it.
b Some people are born evil.
c Sometimes it's difficult to say what's good and what's evil.
d There are no evil people, just bad actions.

9 It's best to be honest because ...
a People respect you more if you're trustworthy.
b My religion tells me so.
c It's usually against the law or the rules to be dishonest.
d I'm happier and feel better about myself if I'm honest.

10 If someone is suffering from an incurable and painful illness, I think that ...
a Everything possible should be done to keep them alive as long as possible.
b It is for God to decide when they should die.
c It's a waste of valuable resources keeping them going, euthanasia is definitely a good thing.
d Quality of life is important, they should be helped to die as painlessly as possible, if that's what they want.

11 Regarding abortion, I believe ...
a In the sanctity of life, so abortionists should be punished as inciting murder.
b Women are entitled to abortion on demand, as a right.
c That we should not play God, so abortion is always wrong.
d Contraception is better, but abortion is preferable to a seriously suffering or unhappy mother or child.

12 Other people matter and should be treated with respect because ...
a God created us all in his image.
b We will all be happier if we treat each other well.
c They are useful to me.
d They are people with feelings like mine.

13   Animals should be treated ...

a   However we see fit – they don't have souls and they
were created for us to use.

b   Kindly because they are sweet and nicer than people.

c   With respect because they can suffer too.

d   With respect because they are part of God's creation.

14   I think we should learn about religion in school because ...

a   Everyone needs religion to make them a better person.

b   It's part of human culture and helps us to understand other people's beliefs.

c   RE is better than History or Science for telling you about the way the world is.

d   I don't think we should learn about religion in school – it's a private matter
for families to teach.

15   I think the holy book of my religion ...

a   Is irrelevant to life today.

b   Contains some truth and is sometimes inspirational.

c   Is inspired by God and literally true.

d   I don't have a holy book, but I find other people's
holy books interesting.

16   I get my ideas about politics and society ...

a   From the teachings of my religion.

b   From television.

c   From my friends and family.

d   By thinking for myself.

17   When something is wrong with the world ...

a   I discuss problems with my friends and family.

b   I ask God to make it better.

c   I think the government should do something about it.

d   I try to do something to improve matters.

18   The most important thing in life is ...

a   To have a good relationship with God.

b   To make lots of money.

c   To preserve the planet for future generations.

d   To increase the general happiness and welfare of humanity.

STUDENT'S PAGE

Answer sheet

Scoring your answers Count how many of each of these symbols you have against your answers: ☺ ☺ ☹ H. Some answers may be shared by people of different viewpoints – if you have two symbols against any answer, count them both in your score.

1	a ☺	b H	c H	d ☺
2	a ☺	b H	c H	d ☺
3	a ☹	b H	c H	d ☺
4	a H	b ☺	c H	d ☺
5	a H	b H	c ☺	d ☺
6	a ☺	b ☺ / H	c ☹	d H / ☺
7	a ☺	b ☺	c H	d ☹
8	a ☺	b ☹	c H / ☺	d H / ☺
9	a H	b ☺	c ☺	d H
10	a ☺	b ☺	c ☹	d H
11	a ☹	b H	c ☺	d H
12	a ☺	b H	c ☹	d H
13	a ☺	b ☹	c H	d ☺
14	a ☺	b H	c ☺	d H
15	a H	b ☺	c ☺	d H
16	a ☺	b ☺	c ☺ / H	d H
17	a ☺ / H	b ☺	c ☺	d H
18	a ☺	b ☹	c H	d H / ☺

☺ 9 – 18
You definitely have a religious faith and would probably find that humanism is not for you, though you may agree with humanists on some issues, especially if you also collected a few H symbols.

☺ 1– 8
You probably have some religious beliefs, but may well decide moral issues on humanist grounds – what were your other answers?

☹ 2 – 8
You don't seem to like people much or to be particularly rational in your views – you're unlikely to be a humanist!

☺ 1 – 7
These answers are fairly neutral, perhaps you are a bit dependent on authority or other people for your opinions.

H 9 – 18
You are a humanist or very close to humanist thinking. Many people are, often without even knowing it! Humanists don't agree about everything, and you may have collected some other symbols too.

H 1 – 8
You may be undecided about your beliefs, or have some religious beliefs combined with a humanist view of moral issues.

The Prisoner's Dilemma

About the game

A deceptively simple game designed to raise the question: 'Why should I, or anyone else, act morally?'

General information

Length of time:	15–20 minutes for the game, 20 minutes for discussion
Group / Class size:	Group size 6–12, even numbers work best, class size unlimited
Materials required:	Playing cards (2 per student), blank sheets of paper, money (ECUs provided on pages 110–112 for optional use). **Note** These instructions have been written for red and black cards, it does not matter what cards you choose, so long as there are two different designs.

Aims

To show that it can be in our own best interest to be selfless and act in a moral way.

How to play

Summary Students play one another at a card game. At the end of the game they add up their points, which may be converted into 'money' for extra incentive. The object of the game is to accumulate as many points as possible.

The set-up The class is divided into groups of up to 12. Each student is given two playing cards, one black and one red, (or other contrasting designs) and must draw up a score sheet by writing the names of the other students in their group on a blank piece of paper.

The card game Students play in pairs within their groups and must play everyone in their group. Keeping in mind the scoring system, they choose a card and place it face down on the table, without letting their opponent see what colour it is. Their opponent does the same. They then turn over the two cards, note down their own scores (see the table on the next page) and pick up their cards. They repeat this process five times. After the fifth time, the players add up their scores and then play the next person in their group. Once they have played everyone in their group they will have a grand total score. (See *Hints and tips* for an example of a scoring sheet.)

How to score

Players score or lose points depending on which colour card they play and what card their opponent plays. The scoring is the most important part of the game and it is crucial that students base their decision about which card to play on the scoring system below. This should be written on the board so it is always visible. At the end of the game students may multiply their scores by ECU 100 (this is essential when playing the alternative version).

THE SCORING SYSTEM

If you play:	and your opponent plays:	you will score:
Black	Black	+3
Black	Red	-2
Red	Black	+5
Red	Red	0

For example, if one player plays a black card, and their opponent plays red, then the first player will lose two points and their opponent will score five points.

At the end of the game Find out which individuals have the top scores and how much each group scored. Point out to the class how much each student and each group *could* have scored if they had all played black cards against one another. This will always be vastly higher than the group scores, and usually it is much higher than any individual score. You should then draw out the implications of the game for social behaviour in general.

The alternative version In order to make clearer the point about black-card playing being the best all-round strategy, you may wish to use this alternative version. Put a pile of ECU notes on the table at the beginning of the game. The exact amount of money should equal:

> 15 × the number in the group (minus one)
> × the total number of students in the class × ECU 100

This represents the amount that the whole class could win if they all played black cards against one another, although don't tell students this until the end of the game.

Let the students play one another in their groups as normal, and count up their scores as normal. When the game is over, each group adds up their total score. Multiply this by ECU 100, and take that amount from the pile, giving it to the groups. When all the groups have got their 'winnings' there should still be a vast amount of money on the table. This is the money they could have won had they not played red cards.

Hints and tips

■ In order to get across the method of playing and scoring, demonstrate a round of five goes with a volunteer. The class should soon get the hang of it.

■ It is crucial that students understand the scoring system and base their decisions on the scoring alone – random 'choices' of cards are not allowed.

■ Students are not allowed to discuss with their opponents their tactics or the cards they are choosing.

■ You should wander round the class checking that students are writing down their scores correctly on the score sheets.

■ Students should write out the names of all the other students in their group on a blank piece of paper. Every round they must write down how many points they themselves scored (ignoring their opponents). After doing this five times they should total up the score then move on to play another opponent and repeat the process until they have played everyone. They should then add up their grand totals. Their score sheet should look something like this:

KEVIN'S SCORE SHEET

Simone	5, -2, 0, 0, 0 = 3
Immanuel	3, 3, -2, 0, 0 = 4
Plato	5, 5, 0, 0, 0 = 10
Soren	-2, -2, 0, 3, -2 = -3
Iris	0, 0, 0, 0, 0 = 0
Thomas	5, 0, 0, 0, 0 = 5

Grand total = 19

Points for discussion

■ What does the game have to do with morality?
This activity can be used to illustrate many issues within moral philosophy. But in order for you to do this students have to make the connection between:

   a selfish action = playing the red card;
and
   a selfless action = playing the black card.

If the game has been understood and played properly then one thing that many students will have realised is that the red card is the potentially higher scoring card, thus:

selfish card versus selfless card – the selfish card wins, the selfless card loses.

Moreover, it also offers less risk as you can never actually lose points; the worst possibility is that you will score zero, but then your opponent will score zero too:

selfish card versus selfish card – no one wins.

The black card on the other hand is the riskier one because it relies on trust – you have to hope that your opponent will play black, and not sting you with a red:

selfless card versus selfless card – both win.

Students who play only red cards are thinking only about themselves; those who play black are considering the overall outcome of the game for both themselves and for their opponent.

■ Why should we be moral?
Because ultimately playing red all the time will lead to failure. This can be shown by inviting students to think about what would happen if this game went on for a long time. The more they play each other, the more they learn to trust and co-operate with black-card players and penalise red-card players. Black-card players will start to do well, red-card players will start to suffer – either they will then leave society or they will learn to play black. And so we could conclude that even in a state of nature, i.e. without any formal government or laws, we have the genesis of altruism – you scratch my back and I'll scratch yours. So why should we be moral? Because in the long run being selfless (playing black) will bring us more benefits than selfishness.

■ Are there similar situations in real life?
To make the point more concrete, you could invite students to think of real-life situations that are similar to the game (e.g. queue jumping). In other words, situations in which it appears to be in our interest to be selfish / immoral, but where the consequence of everyone behaving like this is actually damaging to our self-interest. (This can be linked to the *Universalisability Challenge*, page 65.)

■ What are the origins of morality?
As the points above stress, the origins of morality need not lie in some universal Moral Law, or in the commandments of God. The origins could simply lie in the fact that moral behaviour is more beneficial to the individual, and so, as we all want what's best for ourselves, we act morally. Another possibility is that morality has its origins in the socialisation of individuals by their community. Society benefits from selfless behaviour and so encourages moral behaviour by rewarding it, and punishing selfish behaviour. Yet another possibility is that we have evolved to some extent as moral creatures. Richard Dawkins is one thinker who might take such a line.

■ Can such self-interested behaviour really be called moral?
The game shows that a strong motive we have for being moral (black-card playing) is our own self-interest. But many philosophers have questioned whether behaviour based on self-interest can ever be truly moral. You might invite answers to this question from the class.

■ The game can be used to introduce SOCIAL CONTRACT theory and THOMAS HOBBES. Hobbes thought that humans were innately selfish (red-card players) and that if we lived in a world without governments and laws very few people would prosper. Ultimately it is in our own best interest to give up the freedom we have in a world without laws by signing a contract with our fellows. This contract brings into being a government and laws which will protect us (everyone has to play black) but which will also punish us severely for selfish behaviour (if we play red).

■ Why is it called *The Prisoner's Dilemma?*
The game is based on a well-known scenario used in Game Theory called The Prisoner's Dilemma. Two people are arrested and held in separate cells by the police. The police do not have enough evidence to convict both, and so they make each prisoner the same deal: either the prisoner stays quiet (the black card) or he betrays his friend (the red card). The choices and outcomes are roughly the same as in this game, i.e. the betrayal is the more tempting option (there is the opportunity to go free) and staying quiet requires trust that the other prisoner will stay quiet.

■ You may wish to present the following dilemma to students and ask them to make a decision:
You and your mate are a couple of wide-os, y'know a little bit *Weeah*, a little bit *Woaah*. One night you're casing the joint when all of a sudden, like, the fuzzcops burst in and arrest you for B and E. The dirt though, see they don't have nothing on you. But they separate you from your bro' and make you an offer. 'Either grass your mate up or you keep quiet.' What you both choose to say will determine how much time you each get in the cooler. The Detective Inspector is an expert on logic and points out that:

      If you both confess you both get six years.

      If you both keep quiet you both get one year.

      If you confess and your mate keeps quiet, then you go free and your mate gets ten years.

      But if you keep quiet and your mate confesses then you get ten years and your mate goes free.

What do you do?

10 Universalisability Challenge

About the game

An introduction to the ethical theory of Immanual Kant. Various ethical dilemmas have to be solved using Kant's theory.

General information

Length of time: 15–20 minutes (5 minutes for the exercise, 15 minutes for feedback)

Group / Class size: Group size 2–4, class size unlimited

Materials required: Photocopies of the *Universalisability Challenge* worksheets

---

Aims

To encourage students to think about their own actions in a different way.

To introduce the idea of UNIVERSALISABILITY – or universalising actions through considering a series of dilemmas.

How to play

This activity will not make sense unless you are familiar with Kantian ethics or have read the *Philosophical background* at the end of the exercise.

1 Put the students into groups and give them the dilemma sheets. For each dilemma students should use the following procedure:

   ■ Decide on a course of action.
   ■ Work out the general rule or maxim that they would be following when acting in that way.
   ■ Consider what would happen if everyone followed that rule.
   ■ Only choose a course of action that can be universalised without contradiction.

2 When all the groups have finished, each group should declare how they would act, and talk through their reasoning. They should then consider the strengths and weaknesses of solving moral dilemmas in this way.

Hints and tips

Here is an example of a solution to Dilemma 1 using these rules:

■ First, consider the option of breaking my promise to my nephew. The general rule would be 'Break promises' or 'It's OK to break promises.' (In working out the general rule or maxim we must ignore the specifics of the situation.)

■ What would happen if everyone broke promises? Well, promises would cease to mean anything and would then cease to exist.

■ Breaking promises leads to a contradiction when universalised (as I cannot break something that does not exist) thus I must not break my promise.

Points for discussion

■ Do any of Kant's solutions to moral dilemmas go against our moral intuitions? They might, if we believe that the consequences of an action are as important as the motives for which the duty was done.

■ What should we do when we are faced with two conflicting duties, for example, my duty to keep a promise, but also my duty not to put other people's lives in danger? (This situation arises, as do so many in moral philosophy, when the Mad Axe Murderer knocks on my door asking for the axe I promised he could borrow.)

■ Is there any contradiction in Kant urging us to consider only our duty, and then for him to base our duty on some sort of consequentialist theory about universalising our actions?

■ How can Kant's theory help us to work out how to live our lives? Is everything that is universalisable our moral duty?

Philosophical background

Kant's ethics Kant believed that a good action was one done from the right motive/intention. The only truly good motive is that of duty. An action was good if we did it because we *ought* to have done it and for no other reason.

There are two kinds of 'ought' – those that are conditional on certain desires and wants that we have, and those that are unconditional or absolute. An example of the former would be '*If* I want to get fit then I *ought* to go to the gym'. An example of the latter would be 'I *ought* to keep my promises'. Notice that in the second case there is no 'if', no conditional. Only the unconditional oughts count as moral oughts, and Kant identified morality with keeping to these absolute OBLIGATIONS or duties.

But what are our duties? Kant suggested a way of thinking, a formula that would enable us to work out how to do the right thing. He reasoned like this: when we think that we have done our duty (i.e. done something good) what we mean is that we believe anyone else in the same situation should also have acted in the same way. For example, I may find £50 in a personal letter left in a library book. I decide to send the money and the letter to the rightful owner. I believe I have done the right thing. What this means is that I believe that anyone else in my position should have done the same thing – I believe that we have a duty to return goods to their owners.

So, a good action is one done out of duty. And a duty is something about which we can claim, '*Anyone* in my position should have done that.' In other words, a good action is one that we can *universalise*. Kant thought, from the bare fact that you must be able to universalise good actions, that you could actually work out which actions are good and which bad.

We must be able to universalise our actions if we are to believe we did the right thing. However, we cannot universalise some actions because doing so would lead to a contradiction. These are definitely things we should avoid, and we cannot have a duty to do them. For example: I might have the opportunity to push into a queue. I should then try to universalise my choice – I should ask myself, 'What would happen if everyone pushed into queues?' Well, queues would cease to exist and there would be mayhem. In practice it would be impossible for everyone to jump queues as, if they did, queues would cease to exist – and you cannot push into something that does not exist. Therefore I cannot universalise my decision to jump the queue as in practice it leads to a contradiction. Therefore I should not do it as I should only act in ways that I can wish upon the world generally, in other words, ways that I can legitimately universalise. Thus, as a rational person, I should not push into the queue.

Kant believed that as rational, reasonable humans, we should only act in such a way that we could genuinely apply to all people. To do the right thing is to believe that everyone else in a similar position should do the same thing as well. If the consequences of everyone doing the same thing lead to contradiction, then you cannot be doing the right thing, as you cannot rationally believe that everyone else should do the same thing. As Kant himself says, in what he calls the *categorical imperative*:

> 'Act only on the maxim through which you can at the same time will that it be a universal law.'

Universalisability Challenge

A Using only Kant's theory of ethics, you must decide what would be the right thing to do in each of the following situations.

1 You promise to take your nephew, Johnny, to the park to play on Saturday. But on Wednesday your friend calls up with two tickets for a Cup Final / Cats / Richard Dawkins lecture. Johnny is away camping until Saturday morning. Do you break your promise?

Break promise — Keep promise

2 You are helping your niece, Alice, to do her paper round early so that you can both go and watch a fireworks display. Suddenly the newspaper Alice is holding catches fire in a freak firework accident. Alice is in pain, but there is no water available, only two pints of cold milk on the doorstep of number 32. Do you steal the milk?

Steal milk — Leave milk

3 Your friend who recently developed an eating disorder asks you if her bottom looks lumpy in her new tight trousers. It does. Do you lie?

Lie — Don't lie

4 You are standing on the roof of a building, hauling a piano up to the third floor. Suddenly you hear gunshots. A man on the street directly below the piano is shooting at a passing parade of local dignitaries. Do you drop the piano and kill him?

Drop piano — Hold piano

5 With your partner away working a two-year stint on an oil rig, your very attractive yet terminally ill neighbour confesses undying love for you and asks for one romantic night together before the illness finally takes its toll. You cannot contact your partner. Are you unfaithful?

Be faithful — Be unfaithful

STUDENT'S PAGE

B Now, using only Kant's theory of ethics, decide which of the following actions would be right or wrong to do. Explain how you worked each one out.

1 You are pushing a car up a hill with three other people and you think 'I could just pretend to be pushing, only three people are needed for this job', and so you stop pushing.

   ....

   ....

2 You go to the supermarket to buy some washing powder and buy the own-brand budget powder, because it's slightly cheaper than the environmentally-friendly powder.

   ....

   ....

3 You avoid paying fares on the train, because you know you can get away without paying them.

   ....

   ....

4 You want to listen to some good music, so you borrow a CD from a friend and tape it.

   ....

   ....

5 You cheat in an exam.

   ....

   ....

C Think of your own example of an action that is tempting, but which cannot be universalised.

   ....

   ....

   ....

11 Health or Wealth?

About the game

A team game set in an imaginary hospital. The players have to make tough financial and ethical decisions. The activity is designed to introduce the theory of utilitarianism, and to explore students' own ethical intuitions.

> ### General information
>
> **Length of time:** Approximately 1 hour
> **Group / Class size:** Groups of 3–8 students, class size 8–30
> **Materials required:** Photocopies of the student worksheets and the teacher's blank score sheet, and ECU money, pages 110–112

Aims

To introduce utilitarianism. All the classic problems of the theory are brought out through the various patients' descriptions and dilemmas. As well as encouraging students to think about their own ethical beliefs, the game also requires students to justify their thoughts and opinions.

How to play

The scenario Newtown Hospital is frequently required to make difficult decisions about its patients. It has established an Ethics Committee to help decide which patients should be treated and to help justify these decisions. In this game, the class is divided into teams, each team representing the Ethics Committee working within the hospital.

1 The class is divided into teams of three to eight players.

2 The object of the game is to score the most points. The team with the highest score is the winner. Teams score points by strictly applying and adhering to the principle of utilitarianism. You should award points at the end of each round. (See the scoring sheet, page 74, for instructions on how to score.)

3 There are three rounds in total, although you could choose to do only one or two. For each round, teams are given a photocopied sheet and they must decide both of the following:

■ which of the patients on it should be treated

■ how to resolve the special dilemma

To treat a patient costs money, and each team has only ECU 64,000 to spend. This limits their choices.

4 At the end of each round the team members must be prepared to justify their choices to you.

TEACHER'S PAGE

Before the game – Explain the principle of utilitarianism to the students and write it on the board as a reminder. Explain the rules and hand the money to each team (ECU 64,000 to last all three rounds) along with Sheet 1.

Round One – The teams spend 15 minutes discussing which patients to treat, and how to resolve the Special Dilemma. They must take care to avoid personal prejudices and instead must maintain a strictly utilitarian line in their decisions. Then collect the sheets, along with the money the teams have spent on the patients. The teams must then justify their choices and you can award bonus points. This is at your discretion – if a team defends their choice well you can award them an extra 5–20 points.

Round Two – Give the teams Sheet 2, and while they work on it you should mark Round One using the Suggested Score Sheet on page 74. Every choice, whether or not a patient is treated, has a score attached to it. Add up the scores and announce the scores to the class. After 15 minutes, collect the sheets and money for Round Two, and ask the teams to justify their selections for that round.

Round Three – As Round Two, but at the end total the scores for all three rounds and announce the winner.

Hints and tips

The sheets used in the game are self-explanatory but when explaining the rules it is worth reinforcing these points:

■ The money, ECU 64,000, is designed to last all three rounds. This works out at approximately ECU 21,000 per round, but students are free to spend as little or as much as they want in each round.

■ Tell the students that in this imaginary scenario there are no private hospitals. Patients are either treated at the hospital or they are not treated at all.

■ Students often ask for further details about the patients – tell them that all the available information is on the sheets, and that they must make their decisions on that alone.

■ Have a watch or clock handy and tell the students how long they have left at regular intervals. This helps to keep up the decision-making pressure on the students.

■ **Note 1** Many of the ailments, treatments and costs are not real. Ensure that students are aware of this before the game.

■ **Note 2** The Suggested Score Sheet is simply a suggestion, there are no absolute answers as to what an act utilitarian might say. We have included a blank sheet for you to construct your own scoring system should you wish. (See page 75)

Points for discussion

■ Was the theory easy to apply, or would it have been easier for students to use their own moral intuitions? Students might question whether utilitarianism is the right way to allocate treatment and may like to consider other means or theories, e.g. a 'first come, first serve' rule.

■ Utilitarianism has suffered from many criticisms. Consequently, different forms of utilitarianism have sprung up to avoid various criticisms. Some of the problems you may wish to discuss with your students are outlined here.

■ Very often utilitarianism leads to counter-intuitive outcomes. For example, executing someone who is innocent in order to prevent further crimes seems abhorrent, but a strict utilitarian might advocate it if it maximised happiness. Choosing Trudy Glamour or Kari and Oke are counter-intuitive, but a follower of Bentham might be tempted to save them.

■ Utilitarianism measures consequences, but there are often problems deciding when the consequences of an act finally end. Furthermore how do we actually determine what the consequences of an action are – should we only count the direct consequences, or all the foreseeable consequences? As humans have only finite knowledge of the world we can never know the complete consequences of an action and so, possibly, would never be able to judge whether an action is good or bad. This applies to nearly all the cases in the game.

■ How are we supposed to measure pleasure? Jeremy Bentham had a calculus, a table by which he hoped to calculate the amount of utility an action produced, but it seems that it is impossible to measure a sensation (if pleasure is a sensation). You may like to ask how students would go about quantifying how much pleasure or pain an action produces.

■ Are all pleasures equal? Perhaps some pleasures are inherently better and more valuable than others, even though they may be less pleasant. The last Special Dilemma brings out this problem. Is high culture better than simpler, baser pleasures? Should we aim for a society of happy pigs or unhappy philosophers?

■ Do students think that we should be trying to maximise happiness and pleasure, or to minimise pain? Very often we can't do both and we must choose between the two.

■ Very often we don't have time to think about the consequences of a particular action, but we must make a decision immediately. John Stuart Mill advocates the use of 'secondary principles' or rules based on past experience of what maximises pleasure. This idea has led to the division between act and rule utilitarians. Act utilitarians think we should assess the consequences of each and every particular action before making a decision. Rule utilitarians think we should follow rules (such as 'don't lie', 'don't steal') that if everyone followed would maximise general happiness. For example, in thinking about Special Dilemma 1, an act utilitarian may well use Ms Charman's organs to save others, a rule utilitarian may think that having a 'right to life' as a general rule maximises happiness (everyone feels safer).

■ 'How should pleasure be distributed – over many people, or over a few?' Our answer, and Mill's, would probably be 'over many'. The question then arises: should a few people's pleasure (and possibly their lives, if they are in a coma) be sacrificed for the benefit of the masses? A utilitarian may well say yes, but this fits uncomfortably with our intuitions.

Philosophical background

The theory of utilitarianism is deceptively simple, based on the 'greatest happiness principle'. It claims that:

> A good action is one that maximises general happiness or minimises pain.
> A bad action is one that maximises general pain or minimises happiness.

Consider this simplified example:

A man, Mr X, goes out one night and mugs Mr Y, stealing £50 from him. Is the world a happier place? Well, Mr X has illegally gained £50 and may derive some happiness from this action, say, 10 units of happiness (an arbitrary measure). However, Mr Y will suffer enormously as a result of this. His suffering may last for a long, long time, so he will lose maybe 100 units of happiness. His family and friends may also be badly affected and suffer a loss of, say, 80 happiness points. All in all the action has produced +10 new happiness points but caused –180 points worth of suffering. Overall, the action has increased the suffering in the world and is thus a bad action.

Teacher's Suggested Score Sheet

This sheet suggests the scores you should award to the teams for either choosing to save or to ignore the various individuals. Use this sheet at the end of every round to award points for the patients each team has chosen. For each name circle the score in either the 'Choose' or 'Ignore' column. Also circle the dilemma that each team has chosen. Add up the score and transfer this forward to the next round as a running total.

The example score sheet shows you how to transfer the scores to the team score sheets. In the example, the team has scored a running total of +70 for Round One.

Team name		
PATIENT	SCORE	
	Choose	Ignore
Rebecca Tiller	(+20)	0
Jim Nicholson	+10	(−10)
Henrietta Archman	(+40)	0
Trudy Glamour	+40	(−10)
Catherine O'Shea	−10	(0)
Baby Doe	(−20)	+20
Dilemma	**A**	**B**
	0	(+50)
Running total		+70

(Round One)

Team name		
PATIENT	SCORE	
	Choose	Ignore
Rebecca Tiller	+20	0
Jim Nicholson	+10	−10
Henrietta Archman	+40	0
Trudy Glamour	+40	−10
Catherine O'Shea	−10	0
Baby Doe	−20	+20
Dilemma	**A**	**B**
	0	+50
Running total		

(Round One)

Team name		
PATIENT	SCORE	
	Choose	Ignore
Rebecca Tiller	+20	0
Jim Nicholson	+10	−10
Henrietta Archman	+40	0
Trudy Glamour	+40	−10
Catherine O'Shea	−10	0
Baby Doe	−20	+20
Dilemma	**A**	**B**
	0	+50
Running total		

Team name		
PATIENT	SCORE	
	Choose	Ignore
Kari and Oke	+40	−10
Ben Agyemange	−10	0
'Major' Plum	+10	0
Stephen Spragg	+20	−40
Maria Warlock	0	+20
Withheld	+10	−20
Dilemma	**A**	**B**
	+10	+50
Running total		

(Round Two)

Team name		
PATIENT	SCORE	
	Choose	Ignore
Kari and Oke	+40	−10
Ben Agyemange	−10	0
'Major' Plum	+10	0
Stephen Spragg	+20	−40
Maria Warlock	0	+20
Withheld	+10	−20
Dilemma	**A**	**B**
	+10	+50
Running total		

Team name		
PATIENT	SCORE	
	Choose	Ignore
Bina Choudhury	0	0
Marc Renton	+10	0
Paul Deakin	+30	-10
Jeff Large	+20	-10
Gerard Hoywood	−10	+20
Φ	0	0
Dilemma	**A**	**B**
	+50	+10
Running total		

(Round Three)

Team name		
PATIENT	SCORE	
	Choose	Ignore
Bina Choudhury	0	0
Marc Renton	+10	0
Paul Deakin	+30	-10
Jeff Large	+20	-10
Gerard Hoywood	−10	+20
Φ	0	0
Dilemma	**A**	**B**
	+50	+10
Running total		

TEACHER'S PAGE

Teacher's Blank Score Sheet

Use this sheet to assign your own scores to each patient.

Team name			
	PATIENT	SCORE	
		Choose	Ignore
Round One	Rebecca Tiller	(+20)	0
	Jim Nicholson	+10	(–10)
	Henrietta Archman	(+40)	0
	Trudy Glamour	+40	(–10)
	Catherine O'Shea	–10	(0)
	Baby Doe	(–20)	+20
	Dilemma	A	B
		0	(+50)
Running total		+70	

Team name			
	PATIENT	SCORE	
		Choose	Ignore
Round One	Rebecca Tiller		
	Jim Nicholson		
	Henrietta Archman		
	Trudy Glamour		
	Catherine O'Shea		
	Baby Doe		
	Dilemma		
Running total			

Team name			
	PATIENT	SCORE	
		Choose	Ignore
Round One	Rebecca Tiller		
	Jim Nicholson		
	Henrietta Archman		
	Trudy Glamour		
	Catherine O'Shea		
	Baby Doe		
	Dilemma		
Running total			

Team name			
	PATIENT	SCORE	
		Choose	Ignore
Round Two	Kari and Oke		
	Ben Agyemange		
	'Major' Plum		
	Stephen Spragg		
	Maria Warlock		
	Withheld		
	Dilemma		
Running total			

Team name			
	PATIENT	SCORE	
		Choose	Ignore
Round Two	Kari and Oke		
	Ben Agyemange		
	'Major' Plum		
	Stephen Spragg		
	Maria Warlock		
	Withheld		
	Dilemma		
Running total			

Team name			
	PATIENT	SCORE	
		Choose	Ignore
Round Three	Bina Choudhury		
	Marc Renton		
	Paul Deakin		
	Jeff Large		
	Gerard Hoywood		
	Φ		
	Dilemma		
Running total			

Team name			
	PATIENT	SCORE	
		Choose	Ignore
Round Three	Bina Choudhury		
	Marc Renton		
	Paul Deakin		
	Jeff Large		
	Gerard Hoywood		
	Φ		
	Dilemma		
Running total			

Exploring Ethics   © JOHN MURRAY

STUDENT'S PAGE

Health or Wealth?

Round One   **Newtown Hospital Ethics Committee**

Name	REBECCA TILLER	JIM NICHOLSON	HENRIETTA ARCHMAN
Occupation	Physicist	Artist	Member of Parliament
Age	50	35	47
Diagnosis	Severely damaged retina – blindness imminent	Severely damaged retina – blindness imminent	Weakening of bones
Requirements	**New Optiscope implant – only one available** ←→	**New Optiscope implant – only one available**	**Bone densitometry and physiotherapy**
Cost (ECU)	11,000	11,000	5,000
Details	As an experimental scientist she has taken the country to the forefront of sub-atomic particle research. Without this operation her work will be severely affected.	One of the country's most celebrated artists, he covers his canvases with the contents of randomly stolen dustbins. The patient will no longer be able to work if he loses his sight. Non-urgent case.	The patient has been in a recent scandal, but is on a number of health committees. She has said that she'd be able to 'encourage' funding of the hospital were she to be given priority.
Treat? *Circle your choice*	Yes No	Yes No	Yes No

Name	TRUDY GLAMOUR	CATHERINE O'SHEA	BABY DOE
Occupation	Actress	Personal assistant	N/A
Age	30	54	2 days
Diagnosis	Prematurely ageing skin	Oestrogen deficiency	Down's syndrome with complications
Requirements	**Skin treatment**	**Hormone enhancement therapy**	**Immediate surgery**
Cost (ECU)	10,000	3,000	4,000
Details	Ex-local beauty who has brought happiness to the hearts of generations of movie-goers. Unless she has this treatment it is unlikely she will be employed in the film industry again.	The patient would desperately like to have her first child, and is eager to try this new treatment. Her husband, who has been an orderly at the hospital for 20 years, is also keen to have children.	Baby Doe has a blocked oesophagus and cannot eat or breathe without special equipment. She will die unless treated. Her parents would like her to be kept comfortable and free from pain, but allowed to die naturally.
Treat? *Circle your choice*	Yes No	Yes No	Yes No

✳ ✳ ✳ SPECIAL DILEMMA ✳ ✳ ✳

The organ transplant department have urgently requested the following: 1 × lung; 1 × heart; 1 × liver; 2 × kidney. All of the organs can be supplied by Julia Charman (currently on a life support machine). Should we:

Continue to keep Ms Charman alive on the machine (her chance of recovery is minimal) and so risk losing the lives of those who need transplants? **A**	Allow Ms Charman to die by switching off the machine (six months earlier than normal) and so use the organs to save five other patients? **B**

Starting money   ECU 64,000

Money spent this round   ECU _____

Money left for next round   ECU _____

Exploring Ethics   © JOHN MURRAY

STUDENT'S PAGE

Round Two

Name	KARI AND OKE	BEN AGYEMANGE	'MAJOR' PLUM
Occupation	TV personalities	Poet	Imports and exports
Age	Both 3 years	32	48
Diagnosis	Parasitic skin disease leading to baldness	Kidney failure	Kidney failure
Requirements	**Fur transplant – there are donor cats available**	**Kidney transplant – only one available this month**	**Kidney transplant – only one available this month**
Cost (ECU)	6,000	8,000	8,000
Details	The Blue Peter cats are well-documented as a source of happiness to children everywhere. Producers say the cats will be removed from the programme if the massive hair-loss continues.	A leading poet in his home country, the patient came to England claiming asylum from Nigeria. The Home Office declared him an illegal immigrant. He awaits deportation and an uncertain future.	Freemason and wealthy citizen. The patient grew up in Newtown and makes regular, large donations to local charity. He also employs 10 locals in his business of dealing arms to Nigeria.
Treat? *Circle your choice*	Yes No	Yes No	Yes No

Name	STEPHEN SPRAGG	MARIA WARLOCK	Withheld
Occupation	Unemployed	Unemployed	Unemployed
Age	25	19	28
Diagnosis	Severe damage to legs	Pregnant with triplets	Piece of metal lodged in skull
Requirements	**Extensive reconstruction to avoid amputation**	**Termination of one of the triplets**	**Surgery to prevent permanent brain damage**
Cost (ECU)	11,000	4,000	6,000
Details	Innocent bystander injured in the Burger Bar Bomb. Suspected of dealing soft drugs and found with a small quantity of narcotics on him when he entered hospital. High media interest in his recovery.	The patient, a single mother, is twenty weeks pregnant with triplets and feels she would not be able to cope financially or emotionally with three. She would therefore like to abort one of the fetuses.	The patient is known to be the terrorist responsible for the Burger Bar Bomb. Device detonated early, thus injuring himself and one bystander. Has lived in Newtown for 2 years and has family in Ireland. High media interest.
Treat? *Circle your choice*	Yes No	Yes No	Yes No

---

* * * SPECIAL DILEMMA * * *

It has recently been discovered that a junior doctor has the Hepatitis 'A' virus. Because of the nature of the doctor's work, the chance of any patient having contracted the virus is minimal. Should we:

Announce this to the public, set up a help-line, and a drop-in test clinic for all patients who have had contact with the doctor. This would cause considerable expense to the hospital and stress to the public? A	Keep quiet, taking care not to unnecessarily alarm the public (probably only one or two people out of five thousand have been infected)? B

Money brought forward   ECU _____

Money spent this round   ECU _____

Money left for next round ECU _____

Exploring Ethics © JOHN MURRAY

STUDENT'S PAGE

Round Three

Name	BINA CHOUDHURY	MARK RENTON	Φ
Occupation	Unemployed	Park attendant	Rock goddess
Age	24	25	29
Diagnosis	HIV positive	HIV positive	Minor lesions of the vocal chords
Requirements	**Experimental 'wonder' drug – only one available** ⬌	**Experimental 'wonder' drug – only one available**	**Throat scrapation**
Cost (ECU)	7,000	7,000	13,000
Details	The patient is a haemophiliac and probably contracted the virus through one of the many blood transfusions required to treat her condition.	The patient was a known heroin user and probably contracted the virus through sharing needles. He has been to a drug rehabilitation centre and no longer uses drugs.	The patient has recently lost her trademark gravel voice. She has already called off two concerts, disappointing her thousands of teenage fans. A non-vital operation should rectify this.
Treat? *Circle your choice*	Yes No	Yes No	Yes No

Name	PAUL DEAKIN	JEFF LARGE	GERARD HOYWOOD
Occupation	Professional footballer	X-treme sports instructor	Ex-philosophy lecturer
Age	32	35	31
Diagnosis	Crushed ankle	Ruptured knee ligaments *(again)*	Chronic solipsism
Requirements	**Ankle cartilage realignment**	**ACL reconstruction**	**A sharp dose of reality**
Cost (ECU)	11,000	4,000	3,000
Details	The captain of Newtown F.C. needs this non-necessary operation to get him back to his goal-tastic best. Newtown are having their best ever season and fans are expecting to see some silverware come May.	The patient damaged his knee pulling a 540° Alley-oop to Fakie on his snowboard in Aspen. He finds himself in hospital for the fourth time this year. Unless he has the operation he will be unable to continue his extreme sports instruction.	The patient believes he is the only person in existence, denying the reality of the external world. He lies in bed all day and can no longer look after himself. Although he doesn't specifically refuse treatment, he refuses to acknowledge the existence of the hospital, claiming it is a figment of his imagination.
Treat? *Circle your choice*	Yes No	Yes No	Yes No

---

* * * SPECIAL DILEMMA * * *

The Recreation Department has a spending dilemma. Should they:

Subscribe to a TV soap opera channel for the patients. This popular channel offers a World of Light Entertainment, including many cheap and colourful soaps from Australia and Brazil? A	Invest in a cross-cultural education programme including: plays put on by the staff, a small library of classics and the opportunity to attend lectures on a variety of subjects given by the patients themselves? B

Money brought forward   ECU _____

Money spent this round   ECU _____

Money left for future events ECU _____

TEACHER'S PAGE

12 Costing the Earth

About the game

An enjoyable way of exploring environmental ethics. Teams think up projects to help the environment, which they then try to fund by wheeling and dealing with the rest of the class.

General information

Time required: Approximately 80 minutes

Group / Class size: Groups of 2–3, class size unlimited

Materials required: Money: ECU 20,000 each, see pages 110–112

Aims

To explore the principles behind environmental issues, and to improve students' critical thinking skills through the construction and presentation of arguments.

How to play

Outline the game to students before beginning: students must think of projects that will benefit the environment which they will present to the class at auction. The class must decide which of the other proposals to invest in. The winner is the project that attracts 50% or more of the class investment. In some ways this mirrors the real world of governments and NGOs (Non-Governmental Organisations) which invest limited resources in the future of the environment.

Stage One – Development, about 10 minutes
Divide students into groups of two or three. Groups must then think of global or local environmental projects that would be worth spending money on. Students could think about things that should be banned, conserved, preserved, restored, protected, saved, improved, etc.

Stage Two – Marketing strategy, about 10 minutes
Students prepare a presentation to pitch to the rest of the class to persuade them that their project is worth investing in. The pitch can last no more than two minutes and must include at least one reason why their project is important – this must be related to a value (see *The End Game*, page 24). For example:
1 Rain forests should be saved; this is important because the rain forests produce oxygen; we need oxygen to be healthy; health is something we value.
2 Recycling is important; this is because in the long term it enables us to make more products; this raises our standard of living; our standard of living is something we value.

Students can use any other means of persuasion: rhetoric, sketches, game shows, visual aids, multimedia, etc.

Stage Three – The pitch, about 20 minutes
Groups pitch their projects to the class. Remember: presentations are to be no longer than two minutes, and groups must include at least one reason that is based on a value. You should then write the name of the project and the reasons for supporting it on the board. Repeat this for every group.

Stage Four – The auction, 20 to 30 minutes
Every individual student is now given ECU 20,000. The auction is divided into two or three phases.

a   Pre-auction lobbying – these might be done in a break or in a 15-minute free-for-all, much will depend on the teaching situation and noise levels permissible. Individual students go round the class pitching their ideas and drumming up support for their project. There is opportunity for public appeals to the whole class, and / or for private negotiations, alliances, wheeling and dealing, etc.

b   The bidding – call the class to order and then start the auction. After a quick reminder of each project, students are asked if they want to support that project. If so, they raise their arm holding the amount of money they want to give to the project. A student (one of the project's proposers) then collects all the money and hands the sum to you. This is repeated for all the projects.

Points to remember:

■ Students must give money away – they cannot keep it.

■ Students cannot give money to their own projects.

■ Students act individually in this section, each student is responsible for their own money.

■ Students can give all their money to one project or divide it between many projects as they see fit.

The game can end here. The project with the most money being the winner. Alternatively you can extend the game in this way:

c   If no project has attracted over 50% of the money, then return all the money to the students (everyone is given ECU 20,000). The projects with the least support are eliminated (maybe four or five of them depending on the total number of projects). The remaining groups are allowed 30 seconds to re-pitch the projects and another round of spending ensues. This process is repeated until one project attracts over 50% of the money.

Exploring Ethics   © JOHN MURRAY

Hints and tips

■ The presentations are the key. Students can use any means they consider necessary, except intimidation. Encourage students to be imaginative.

■ Presentations must be kept strictly to the time allowed.

■ Students should be quiet during other presentations.

■ When the groups give their presentations you should seek clarification of reasons: What's so valuable about rain forests? Is the environment important in itself? Or is it important for instrumental reasons, e.g. because it is important to other species, or human beings? What kind of importance?

■ Give a two-minute warning before the end of each phase to give students a chance to finish.

Points for discussion

■ What reasons were given for a particular project being valuable or important? Is every environmental concern ultimately based on a value? Do all these values come down to the same thing?

■ What difficulties were there in choosing and prioritising the projects?

■ Why did a project win, or why was it difficult to choose a clear winner?

■ How were student decisions reached? What, if anything, persuaded them to change their minds? Were rhetoric or friendship more influential than reason?

■ The underlying principles of choice – are there any general principles which can be applied to environmental issues? For example, avoidance of cruelty, aesthetics, concern for future generations.

■ What would students be prepared to do, or to give up, to put their principles into action?

13 Planet Thera

About the game

A good format for discussing various political and social issues. Students have to agree a set of rules to live by in a new life on another planet.

General information

Length of time: 30 minutes
Group / Class size: Group size 6, class size unlimited
Materials required: Photocopies of the student worksheets

Aims

To encourage students to think about a variety of political issues, in particular what kind of society they would like to live in and what sort of laws they would like to live under.

How to play

Scenario With the Earth becoming uninhabitable, the Government has decided to transport people to a new life on another planet – Thera. Unfortunately, the Transmorpher that is used to send people to Thera has its limitations – people arrive there with different bodies. Planet Thera has been divided up into different zones, each with its own social rules, and the Government has insisted that before groups go they agree on the social rules they want to live by. Each group will then be sent to the zone that matches their rules.

Just how primitive is the Transmorpher? Well, in order to be transported to Thera you go into a Neuro-Scanner where your brain is 'read' by a computer. This information is then sent in digital form across the universe to a Reconstructer on Planet Thera that uses organic matter to rebuild your brain. Your new brain is then randomly assigned one of six pre-prepared bodies. So, although your brain will be the same, your body will be different.

The six types of bodies that students could find themselves with are outlined on the *Species specification sheet*.

1 Divide the class into groups. Give each group the *Species specification sheet* and tell them that it should be referred to throughout the discussion.
2 Tell students that the aim of the game is to come up with fair and workable rules that they all agree to live by in their new lives. In order to focus the discussion, you may wish to assign a different topic to each group. Topics can be selected and adapted to suit the needs of the class, but may include:

- Family, children, education
- Division of labour, rewards for labour
- Welfare of needy, health care
- Property – individual or communal? – taxation
- Life and death – euthanasia, abortion
- Justice – crime and punishment
- Organisation of society – leadership, elections, democracy
- The environment, relationships with other species

3　Students must now work out the relevant rules that they are going to live by. Remember – they do not know in advance what kind of body they are going to have.

4　At the end of the discussion period, students should report back to the class on the rules they have chosen.

Hints and tips

- Planet Thera is in many ways like Earth. It is habitable, there is oxygen and water, the climate is mild, days are 24 hours long, and vegetable and animal species exist that are capable of sustaining human life.

  To vary or extend the discussion, you might want to tell students that water (or any other resource) is in scarce supply.

- In theory, what should evolve is a fairly egalitarian system, because everyone is potentially one of the more vulnerable members of society. In practice, students may be more confident, happier to take risks, and may choose a more competitive model for their society. They may need to be reminded that they are not arguing from their personal perspective, because they cannot know in advance what kind of characteristics they will have.

Points for discussion

- These are the rules students would like to live by on Planet Thera but are they the same as the ones students would like to live by on Earth? One of the purposes of this exercise is to invite students to think of society from a position other than their own. We all have our own selfish interests, and might all like to live in a society where the rules favour us, i.e. a society in which we are particularly privileged or respected or rewarded. The problem is that we can't all be favoured above everyone else, for then we would all be equal! It seems that we have a choice in the kind of society we would like to live in. Either it would be one in which selfish interests are put to one side, and everyone is treated equally, or it would be a society which is biased towards the selfish interests of a few.

- What would a just society be like? Is this game a good way of working out the rules of a just society? JOHN RAWLS thought so – he came up with a thought experiment called the Original Position in which he asks us to imagine that we are under a *veil of ignorance*. We do not know what our sex is, or our race, our age, our abilities, our class or socio-economic standing. From this Original Position we must work out the principles, rules and laws of a society that we would like to live in. Rawls thought that everyone put behind this veil of ignorance would come up with the same two basic principles of justice. Firstly, the right for everyone to have as much freedom as is compatible with the freedom of others; secondly, the principle that there is equality of opportunity and that any inequalities that arise in society are justifiable only insofar as they benefit the worst off.

■ Can there be too many laws? If we have too many laws and duties then there will be less freedom, as we have to obey these laws, as well as pay taxes to enforce the laws, provide free health, education, organisation, etc. John Stuart Mill believed that society had too many laws, to the extent that they interfered with the thing we most care about – our freedom to pursue our own goals. He argued that we only really need one principle – that we should never harm others. In other words we should be free to do whatever we like, and the only laws should be to prevent us causing harm to others.

■ Can there be too few laws? Some philosophers have criticised Mill by saying that it is true that Mill's system (with minimal government interference) will give us freedom, but it is the wrong sort of freedom. It is easy to imagine a society governed by Mill's principle, in which there were extremes of wealth. Sure, the poor of such a society would be free from interference, but if they had no money then they would not be able to do anything. What kind of freedom is that? We need laws to help the poorest and most disadvantaged so that they have a more positive kind of freedom, a freedom to pursue their own goals.

■ Do we have natural rights? Many students might want to claim certain rights on Thera – the right to free speech, the right to clean air, the right to defend themselves by violence. Many philosophers (e.g. Jeremy Bentham) have argued that there is no such thing as a natural right, and that the only rights that exist are civic rights – ones that have been laid down in the form of a contract or law. Each right will have a corresponding duty, and the rights become established in law by making the duty a legal requirement.

For example, a right to clean air becomes a duty on behalf of everyone not to pollute the air, such a duty may become a law. Or a right to free education entails a duty on behalf of society to provide such an education, and in turn this may require certain taxes to pay for it.

As an exercise, you might ask students to convert any 'rights' that they have written down into corresponding duties and laws.

The set-up

It's the year 2520. Due to global warming, Earth is no longer inhabitable by human beings. A group of six of you have been selected to join the new colonies on Planet Thera. To get there you must take the Transmorpher.

The Transmorpher

In order to be transported to Thera you must go through a Neuro-Scanner where your brain is 'read' by a computer. This information is then sent in digital form across the universe to a Reconstructer on Planet Thera that uses organic matter to rebuild your brain. Your new brain is then randomly assigned one of six pre-prepared bodies (see the *Species specification sheet*). So although your brain will be the same on Planet Thera, your body will be different.

The task

Thera has been divided into different zones according to the different rules that are enforced in each zone. To avoid conflict, the Government has insisted that you work out what social rules you want to live by before entering Thera. *Your group's task is to work out what rules you want to live by on Thera.* When you get there you will be assigned to the zone that has rules that match yours. You will live there for the rest of your life.

Remember: on Planet Thera you do not know what kind of body you are going to have.

Species specification sheet

APPEARANCE: 5–6ft, purple, hairless

AGE: 19–29

RACE: Gamenes

SEX: hermaphrodite

STRENGTHS: quick and agile

WEAKNESSES: cannot survive the cold

APPEARANCE: 6–8 ft giants, orange

AGE: 50–80

RACE: Citroids

SEX: male or female

STRENGTHS: can see ultraviolet and infrared light

WEAKNESSES: needs to drink 10 litres of water per day

APPEARANCE: 3–4 ft, blue, hairy

AGE: 4–13

RACE: K/we

SEX: male or female

STRENGTHS: need very little sustenance to survive

WEAKNESSES: prone to infectious diseases

APPEARANCE: 5 ft, bright red, 4 or 6 arms

AGE: 13–18

RACE: Ilenquods

SEX: male or female

STRENGTHS: the extra limbs have obvious advantages

WEAKNESSES: virtually blind

APPEARANCE: 5ft, green with bulbous forehead

AGE: between 80–120

RACE: Vesuvian ingot

SEX: male or female

STRENGTHS: excellent manual dexterity

WEAKNESSES: physically weak

APPEARANCE: 7ft, gold and silver

AGE: 30–40

RACE: Cyborg mk VIII

SEX: not applicable

STRENGTHS: extremely strong

WEAKNESSES: requires weekly blood transfusion to survive

14 There Are No Laws

About the game

A simple exercise based on an imaginary scenario in which laws are suddenly abolished.

General information

Length of time: 20–30 minutes
Group / Class size: Students work individually, class size unlimited
Materials required: A blank piece of paper and pen for each student

---

Aims

To encourage students to think about what a world without laws would be like. To explore the relationship between morality and the need for social rules.

How to play

1 Read out the following scenario in the dramatic style of a newsreader announcing a sudden newsflash:

> Helicopters suddenly appear above this classroom and announce the following news:
>
> There are no more laws. Repeat: all laws have been abolished. Any action you perform will have no legal consequence as there are no laws. There will be no police or military as there are no laws to enforce. This applies as of now and applies throughout the world.
>
> All over the world similar announcements are being made. There are no more laws, no legal system, no courts, no police, no parliament, no punishment, no crimes – as of now.

2 Students should think about answers to the following questions and write them down. Given that there are no more laws:

   a What would you do in the next ten minutes?
   b What would you do over the next few days?
   c What would be your long-term plan?
   d What would happen to conventional morality?
   e Who do you think would rise to the top?

   Students should be allowed some discussion with their neighbours, but their final answers should be their own.

3   Go through each of the questions, discussing each one in turn. Invite students to read out some of their answers, to the general amusement of all.

Hints and tips

■ When students read out their answers you must help them think about whether or not their answers are realistic. For example someone might say: 'I'd get loads of guns, steal a helicopter and become ruler of Britain,' but on further questioning this is shown to be an absurdly unrealistic series of actions. The last place to go to if laws were abolished would be a gun shop as this would almost certainly lead to death.

Again, if a student says 'I'd go into hiding in the country,' you might ask where, how they'd get there, and how they think they'd survive.

If a student says 'I'd ram-raid a shop and steal a huge TV,' you might ask whether there would be any workers left to supply the electricity.

Points for discussion

■ Would it be possible to get out of a big city? Would money still exist? Would anyone go to work? Would there be any trains / buses / public services? Would there be wide-scale panic? How long would this last? What would the army do?

This exercise could be related to Thomas Hobbes' concept of a 'state of nature', in which our lives would be 'nasty, brutish and short'. Do students think there would be widespread killing and viciousness, or would most people struggle to get on as normal? Does such a scenario reveal anything at all about 'human nature'?

■ One of the more interesting questions is to think of what kind of morality might develop. Would it be the law of the jungle in which 'might is right', and would those with guns and terror behind them eventually take control?

15 Just a Minute

About the game

Based on one of Plato's famous dialogues, this is a play with a difference, giving students the opportunity to act, argue and think all at the same time.

> ### General information
>
> **Length of time:** 25–30 minutes
> **Group / Class size:** This works best with a single group of 10-20 students
> **Materials required:** Copies of the *Just a Minute* dialogue; buzzers or bells if possible

Aims

To introduce students to the critical analysis of arguments by looking at the SOCRATIC DIALOGUE method of discussion. To introduce different ways of thinking about justice.

How to play

Scenario The scene is Ancient Athens, 2,500 years ago. Socrates & Co. are having yet another argument about the nature of morality, in this case: 'What is justice?' They are surrounded by a flock of admirers who are eager to join this band of philosophical desperadoes. In order to become one of Socrates' groupies, the admirers must show that they have understood his DIALECTICAL method. Their aim is to score points by catching out the disputants and so impress Socrates with their philosophical abilities.

1 Divide students into groups:
   a The *Characters*, who are to take the roles of Socrates and his friends. (These can be changed around to give several students a chance to read.) These characters also double up as the *Judges*, who will adjudicate the *Contestants'* challenges.
   b Two or more teams of *Contestants*, who form the audience (about four to six students per team). They will each be attempting to catch the *Characters* out as they argue.
2 Give a copy of the *Just a Minute* dialogue to all the readers, plus one or two copies to each team of contestants.
3 The *Characters* start to read the dialogue aloud as if it were a normal play, though they can choose to put in whatever actorly flourishes they like in order to sound convincing. They must stop reading, however, as soon as there is a challenge.
4 The aim of the *Contestants* is to score points for their team and they do this by successfully challenging the characters. Ideally the contestants should have buzzers or bells which they can hit to make challenges. In the absence of bells, students can simply bang the table.

5 Challenges may come at any time, but can only be of the following four types, so contestants should be looking out for:

a Conclusions – When a *Character* seems to have completed an argument. *Contestants* should look out for words like 'therefore'.

b Leading or RHETORICAL questions – When a *Character* asks a question to which they obviously know the answer, but they ask it anyway.

c Analogies or examples – When a *Character* draws a comparison with something else or uses a concrete situation to make their point.

d Sarcastic remarks – A very crude method of making the opponent look stupid.

6 When a challenge has been made, the *Judges* invite the *Contestant* to explain what the challenge is, why they have made it, and at what line it occurs. They then vote on whether it was a legitimate challenge. You should award points as follows:

> Conclusion – 10 points
> Leading or rhetorical questions – 7 points
> Analogies or examples – 5 points
> Sarcastic remarks – 3 points

Note A challenge may not be made until the characters have actually spoken the relevant words, i.e. challenges cannot be made in advance.

Hints and tips

■ The challenges should be written on the board to remind the *Contestants* of the kinds of interruptions they may make.

■ Cough surreptitiously when you think either team has missed an obvious conclusion or leading question.

■ The groups could change around for the three different parts of the dialogue, giving everyone a chance to challenge and act.

Points for discussion (See also *Socrateaser*, page 98)

■ Plato used Socrates as the main character in nearly all of his philosophical plays (known as 'dialogues'). In these dialogues Socrates discusses with other Greek characters the meaning of moral concepts, like goodness, justice and virtue. In this dialogue (based on Book I of the *Republic*) the question 'What is justice?' is raised.

■ For Plato, as for many Greeks, justice was a virtue (an excellence) possessed by humans who were virtuous in other respects. In particular for Plato, justice existed in those people who encouraged reason and wisdom to rule their lives. Is justice still thought of as a kind of disposition or 'personality trait' or do we now think of it as something different, something external?

■ What do students think justice is? Have any of the characters got it right? For example, is it about paying your dues, being fair to friend and foe alike? Students might like to think about different kinds of justice, and the purposes of justice. Is justice about punishment / revenge / correction / fairness?

■ Plato made a clear distinction between two ways of arguing: that of Socrates and that of the SOPHISTS. The Socratic method relied on giving reasons for a belief, on analysing terms, on searching for criteria and on finding the truth. In contrast, the Sophists were interested in persuading their audience by whatever means necessary, often resorting to browbeating or emotional rhetoric to win the audience over. An interesting side issue is whether Socrates ever resorts to the methods he so despises in his opponents.

Just a Minute

The Dialogue

The characters, in order of appearance:

Narrator	The wise and friendly teacher
Socrates	The leading character, a skilful and charismatic debater
Cephalus	A rich businessman, in the twilight of his years
Glaucon	Plato's elder brother, a man of few words
Polemarchus	Cephalus' son, the voice of the common people
Thracymachus	A cynical old man, skilled in the art of rhetoric

Part One

Narrator	*Socrates and his friends are relaxing on the cool marble patio of Polemarchus' mansion – they've had a long and hard day at the festival. The vines fall rich with their bounty around the pillars. It's a Greek summer evening and there's nothing to do but talk. We catch them in mid-dialogue ...*
Socrates	(*a skilful and charismatic debater*) You're looking very good these days, Cephalus. Tell us, what's your secret?
Cephalus	(*in the twilight of his years*) Nice of you to say so, Socrates, you little charmer you. It's true, old age is treating me kindly.
Socrates	There's plenty who'd put that down to the fact that you're one of the richest men in Athens. Not that I bear any grudges – at least you're not obsessed with money like some people I know.
Cephalus	I've always said money is worth nothing without good character.
Socrates	True, true ... Look Cephalus, I've always wanted to ask you, what's the best thing about being so rich?
Cephalus	Actually, it's not what you'd expect. It's not the endless parties, the wine, the fact you can have anything you want. No, nothing like that. Because when you're facing the prospect of death you start to worry about other things.
Glaucon	(*a man of few words*) What on earth have you got to worry about? You're loaded ...

STUDENT'S PAGE

Cephalus   I have nothing on earth to worry about. People say that when we die we will be judged and the good will be rewarded and the bad punished. So I think to myself 'I'd better make sure I've been a good man, paid my debts, told the truth,' and so on. Well, Socrates, do you know the price of sacrifices these days? Have you heard how much they're charging for entrails down at the Oracle? It's outrageous – 50 drachma for some scrawny chicken giblets! And another thing, the price of feta ...

Socrates   Anyway, you were saying, because you are rich ...

Cephalus   Oh yes, yes. Because of my modest fortune I can afford to pay my debts, both to the gods and to society. The way I see it is this: I'm a simple man, but so long as I've told the truth and given back what I owe in this life, then I'll be seen as a just man in the next – and so escape punishment.

Socrates   Hold on. I've always been interested in finding out what justice is, and you seem to have come up with an answer. Did you say that being just* simply means giving back what you've borrowed and telling the truth?

Cephalus   I did.

Socrates   Hmm, let's think about this. So if I borrow your ceremonial chariot and refuse to give it back, then that's unjust. Furthermore, if I gave it back to you and said I'd treated it with great respect, whereas really I'd been using it to impress the youths in the market place, then my lie would also be unjust.

Cephalus   Two excellent examples, proving my point exactly.

Socrates   But what about this? Suppose an acquaintance lent you an axe, and subsequently it is rumoured he went mad. Then one dark night he knocks at your door, foaming at the mouth and asks for his axe back, muttering to himself 'Mad they said ... I'll show them ... Oh yes, I'll show them alright ... let's see if they laugh at me now ...' Are you saying it would be right to give him back his axe?

Cephalus   I may be old, Socrates, but I'm not senile yet. Of course that wouldn't be right.

Socrates   Even though you had in fact borrowed the axe from him and he was asking for it back?

Cephalus   No, I'd even lie to him if necessary. The only way we're ever going to stop these Mad Axe Murderers is to prevent them from getting hold of axes in the first place.

Socrates   So on the one hand you're claiming that returning what you borrow and telling the truth is the just and right thing to do. But on the other hand

* Socrates uses the word 'just' in the way we often use the word 'moral', i.e. to refer to those people and actions that are morally good.

Exploring Ethics   © JOHN MURRAY

you're saying that sometimes refusing to return what you've borrowed and lying is the right thing to do. I don't like to point this out Cephalus, but you've completely contradicted yourself.

Cephalus   Er ... Look Socrates, I'm a bit distracted this evening, we drank a lot of wine at the festival, and my head's beginning to hurt.

Socrates   No need to apologise my friend, I'm glad we cleared this up. I think we can conclude our little discussion by agreeing that telling the truth and returning what you've borrowed isn't the correct definition of justice.

Polemarchus   (*the voice of the common people*) I disagree, and I can show you why you, Socrates, are mistaken and my father is indeed correct.

Cephalus   My son, I'm bored with all this talking. I'll let you two layabouts carry on the argument yourselves, you seem to have nothing better to do. I've got to go and see a man about a sacrifice.

Socrates   Some people just don't take philosophy seriously enough.

Glaucon   (*a man of few words*) One day they'll learn.

Part Two

Narrator   *Glaucon's words turned out to be almost prophetic. For when Cephalus died, the Athenian government confiscated his land and riches, and refused to give it to Polemarchus to whom it was due. But this is to stray from the story, and we must return to our friends and their noble quest for the truth.*

Socrates   Polemarchus, as heir to this argument you must tell us what justice really is. Because we would all like to know.

Polemarchus   I think we can learn from the wise man, Simonides about this matter. He said:

'It's the right thing to do
to give everyone their due.
And when money is in lieu
pay your friend, 'ere you rue.' †

Socrates   A moment please. (*Socrates chokes back a tear.*) I'm truly moved by such beauty. Obviously Simonides wrote some fine poems in his time, but judging by this one they weren't very philosophical. For if your great poet is right, Polemarchus, then surely the Mad Man is owed his axe and we should give it back to him.

† Poetic licence!

Polemarchus	No, no, no. You're missing the point. 'Giving everyone their due' isn't just about possessions, it's about being good to your friends, and harming your enemies. In other words giving people their due.
Socrates	Ah, so that's what he meant. Couldn't he just have come out and said it in plain Greek? So justice means giving to people what we think is appropriate for them, whatever that is.
Polemarchus	Yes, and as I've just told you, that means helping our friends, the people we think are good, and harming our enemies, those we think are bad. Do you see what I'm getting at?
Socrates	Oh, you know how ignorant I am of these things, Polemarchus. I'm just asking a few innocent questions, keeping the conversation going, that sort of thing. But here's a thought, do you think that it could ever be just to actually harm our friends, or even, dare I say it, help our enemies?
Polemarchus	If I didn't know you better, I'd swear you were trying to irritate me by asking me such questions and pretending you didn't know how I was going to answer.
Thracymachus	(*skilled in the art of rhetoric*) I'll tell you what, he's irritating me alright, that's for sure. One day Socrates you're going to get an almighty kicking – and that's something that's due, in fact it's *over*due.
Socrates	Pray tell, Thracymachus, you and whose army? But, I apologise, we must avoid such rhetoric. Our sophisticated friend here has given us an excellent example. So, Polemarchus, do you think that I should be given an 'almighty kicking' – would that be just?
Polemarchus	Not at all, because you are clearly a good man. And it can never be right to harm good men.
Socrates	Tell me Polemarchus, do we ever mistake a good man for bad and vice versa?
Polemarchus	Of course, we all make mistakes. But where is all this leading, Socrates?
Socrates	Well, my friend, correct me if I'm wrong, but didn't you say that justice means helping and harming those people we think are good and bad?
Polemarchus	Neither of us is deaf!
Socrates	And so by your reckoning sometimes it is right to help a bad man (because we think they're good), and it's also right to harm a good man (because we think they're bad). Yet I distinctly remember you also saying that it is never just to harm someone good. You seem to be contradicting yourself. What would your poet say now?
Polemarchus	Doh! What a fool I've been Socrates, I must have been mistaken about the definition.

Socrates	You know what – I think you were. Therefore it wasn't a wise man that said that justice means giving everyone their due. But the problem is we still don't know what justice is.

Part Three

Narrator	*Polemarchus spoke with the voice of the common people, who believe it is just to harm those we think are bad. In a tragic and ironic twist of history, Polemarchus himself fell victim to this distorted view of justice: he was murdered by the Athenian government when it confiscated his father's lands.*
Thracymachus	I've had enough of this tripe you've been talking, Socrates. Just listen to yourself, you pathetic man. You babble on like a baby with all your polite questions: 'Oh pray, do tell me Polemarchus, don't you agree that it isn't the case that Axe Men in chariots are people we think we think are bad, but we really think are good.' Utter rubbish. Why don't you just tell us what you think justice is or shut up?
Socrates	Don't be hard on us, Thracymachus. We are ignorant folk, and clever chaps like you ought to feel sorry for us instead of getting irritated.
Thracymachus	There you go again Socrates. Playing to the gallery, getting everyone on your side, as if that will bring us nearer to the truth.
Socrates	You can see right through me, can't you?
Thracymachus	Tell us all, my wise friend, what you think justice is. And don't say 'It's duty or advantage or profit'. I want a precise definition.
Socrates	Hah! You ask someone for a definition of '12' and add 'But don't tell me it's 2 times 6, or 3 times 4, or 7 plus 5'. How do you want me to answer – by lying? I'll tell you what, if you can tell me the right definition, then I shall heap a thousand praises on you.
Thracymachus	You know that I can't teach you without money up front.
Socrates	I'll give it to you when I have the cash.
Glaucon	We'll pay for you Socrates. Go on then, Thracymachus, give us your answer.
Thracymachus	Listen then. I say that justice is simply whatever is in the interests of those who have power. Anything that helps them keep their power is called 'just', and there's nothing more to it than that. Now where's your praise?

Socrates	You'll have it when I understand what you're talking about. Are you saying that Glaucon here, because he has the biggest muscles and is the most powerful, determines what justice is? I'm sure that eating lots of eggs keeps him powerful, but are you claiming that justice consists in egg-eating?
Thracymachus	Don't be tiresome, you're deliberately misunderstanding me. By 'power' I meant political power of course, in other words the rulers of a state. So justice means obeying the laws of a state, and those laws are simply there to keep the rulers in power.
Socrates	I'm shocked. I thought justice meant doing the right thing.
Thracymachus	You're so naïve, Socrates. Do you really think there is anything more to being just apart from doing what you're told? I say that you're actually better off ignoring the laws and morals of society and doing what you can to get what you want. If that means being unjust, then so be it.
Socrates	Let's go back a bit. Firstly – do you think a ruler can ever make mistakes about what's in their interest?
Thracymachus	Yes, after all, to err is human.
Socrates	In which case their laws aren't always just, as you've defined it, because the rulers may pass laws which are actually against their interest. Secondly, do you think that a law can ever be unjust – for example a law that banned sophists like you from speaking in public?
Thracymachus	I'm rapidly losing interest, Socrates, get on with your intellectual games.
Socrates	Well, if you agree with what I've just said then we can conclude that there's more to justice than 'whatever is in the interest of the rulers' and you, my dear Thracymachus, are wrong.
Thracymachus	Tell me, Socrates, do you have a nurse?
Socrates	What do you mean?
Thracymachus	Well, she let's you go drivelling round without wiping your nose, and you can't even tell her the difference between a sheep and a shepherd.
Narrator	*Some of these ancient jokes are lost in translation, but despite this the argument goes on long into the Mediterranean night ...*

16 Socrateaser

About the game

Students imitate the style of Plato, and construct their own philosophical works of genius.

General information

Length of time: 30 minutes (5 to read the example, 25 to write the dialogue)

Group / Class size: Groups of 3 students, class size unlimited

Materials required: Copies of the *Socrateaser* worksheet, pen and paper

Aims

This is an exercise in critical thinking. By attempting to define a concept, students learn in more detail one of the standard methods of criticising an argument.

How to play

Background Nearly all Plato's philosophical works take the form of a dialogue between Socrates and several other characters who engage in discussion and debate with him. Plato's later books tend to be long monologues in which he uses Socrates, and sometimes other characters, as a mouthpiece for his theories. But the early works of Plato are like plays in which Socrates uses a specific kind of dynamic argument that has come to be known as the DIALECTIC.

Ideally the class should be familiar with *Just a Minute*, on page 89, as it provides them with a short example of the Socratic style of dialogue and debate.

1 Run carefully through the *Socrateaser* worksheet with the students. Before they can write a Socratic dialogue, students need to look at some of the essential elements that might be included.

2 Divide students into groups of three. Each group has to construct a Socratic dialogue using Socrates and at least one other character. Students can refer to the example given, but remind them of the crucial steps by reading out the following checklist:

a Pick some characters to argue with Socrates.

b Choose a concept from those mentioned on the sheet, or pick anything you like, although not 'pens'.

c Let one of the characters offer a preliminary definition of the concept.

d Then have Socrates give a counter-example. Something that is obviously an example of X, but does not fulfil the initial definition of X. Socrates can now reject this definition.

TEACHER'S PAGE

    e Let another character offer a better definition of X, and then use Socrates to criticise that.

    f Remember to be sarcastic sometimes, and to have people agreeing with Socrates in a fairly bored way.

Hints and tips

■ Students may want to try to define objects rather than concepts, and although this is easier, it is not as interesting.

■ It is important to help groups with their dialogues, especially in the definitions and the counter-examples to them.

Points for discussion

■ For those students who are interested in the technical aspects of the argument, this is how the first of Socrates' counter-examples works:
— Mr Hayward has claimed that all As (pens) are Bs (things you use to write).
— Socrates then gets Mr Hayward to agree that C (an empty pen) is an A (a pen) but that C is not a B (because we cannot write with it).
— The problem is that Mr Hayward's definition is that all As are B, yet here is an A that is not a B. So Mr Hayward's definition must be wrong.

■ Socrates constantly used this and similar methods of argument in his debates: this method is known as the ELENCHUS. He would force people to question their beliefs by showing how they lead to contradictions. Socrates was one of the first philosophers to argue purely by using logic, and not using emotional arguments or employing fancy sound-bites and spin. Socrates preached reason over rhetoric.

■ One aspect of a Socratic dialogue is the way in which Socrates invites everyone to suggest a definition, and then shows each of them to be inadequate in some way. Ideally, what should happen is that each definition is a better version of each preceding definition, as the listeners learn from their mistakes. We may call this *finding the criteria or specifications for the concept being debated.*

Note Socrates never claims to have knowledge of the things he's talking about, his point is to show us that those of us who think we have knowledge haven't thought hard enough about the subject. As his questioning goes on you get the feeling that you are getting nearer and nearer a reasonable definition. Unfortunately, not all of his arguments are convincing, and it is only in the monologues of his later works that Plato, using Socrates, gets near to persuading us of his theories.

STUDENT'S PAGE

Socrateaser

This is your chance to write a philosophical masterpiece.
All you have to do is to read the example below,
follow the simple instructions as you go, and then get writing.

Step 1 The first thing to do is to choose a concept that you wish to analyse or define. For Plato these included Beauty, Wisdom, Truth, Love, Knowledge, Justice, Courage, Belief. Alternatively, you might want to look at things like Happiness, Perfection, Friendship, Duty, Society, or the Soul. The initial question comes in the form 'What is ...?'

Socrates   *Can anyone tell me what a pen is?*

Step 2 In response one of the characters offers an initial definition, perhaps the first thing that comes to their mind, or a common-sense notion that they haven't really thought through:

Mr Hayward   *A pen is that which you write with.*

Step 3 Socrates then destroys the definition with a counter-example, an object that blatantly is a member of the class being defined (in this case a pen) but which does not fulfil the definition:

Socrates   *A fine definition. But tell me, Mr Hayward, do you see this thing here. What's this? (Socrates holds up a pen.)*

Mr Hayward   *What trick is this? It's a pen of course.*

Socrates   *Could you please autograph my toga.*

Mr Hayward   *Of course.* (He tries to write with it.) *I can't use this – it's empty.*

Socrates   *What's empty?*

Mr Hayward   *The pen.*

Socrates   *But that can't be a pen.*

Mr Hayward   *What do you mean?*

Socrates   *Well, a moment ago you said that a pen was that which you write with. But as you can't write with the thing you're holding, it can't be a pen. Therefore either your definition is wrong, or it literally isn't a pen. Personally I think your definition is wrong. Do you agree?*

Step 4 The other characters, when they have been beaten at any stage of the argument tend to end up agreeing with Socrates in a very grovelling manner.

Mr Hayward   *Yes, Socrates you are right.*

Step 5 Another character then proposes a better definition and the whole process is repeated.

Mr Jones	*I know the answer Socrates. Any object that did, does or will emit ink is a pen.*

Step 6 Socrates refutes the new definition by asking a series of leading and distracting or seemingly irrelevant questions, to which his listener invariably agrees. Socrates' flattery puts the listener at his ease, making him more amenable to giving Socrates the replies he wants. Finally Socrates springs the trap and shows that the speaker has *contradicted* what he originally said.

Socrates	*So everything that emits ink is a pen.*
Mr Jones	*Yes, that's right.*
Socrates	*And do you know of the animal that lives at the depths of the sea that has eight legs?*
Mr Jones	*You mean an octopus.*
Socrates	*I do not know how I am going to win an argument against someone so clever, Mr Jones, but let me try! I don't suppose you know how an octopus defends herself, for surely only a marine biologist would know that.*
Mr Jones	*I do know that Socrates. It is by squirting ink into the face of the attacker.*
Socrates	*Once again I am impressed. Now would you say this ink was emitted?*
Mr Jones	*Of course, for how else would you describe the escape of the liquid from her body.*
Socrates	*Now I'm sure you know the answer to my next question, unless you have had an accident and hurt your head.*
Mr Jones	*I have not had an accident. So, what is your next question, for I am ready?*
Socrates	*Is an octopus a pen?*
Mr Jones	*Obviously not.*
Socrates	*But it must be for it emits ink which is the definition of a pen. Unless of course your definition is wrong.*
Mr Jones	*I think perhaps it is. But tell me, oh wise Socrates, what do you think a pen is?*
Socrates	*I have no idea.*

Step 7 Remember to inject your dialogue with a healthy dose of sarcasm and humour.

Mr Jones	*Perhaps we could say that a pen is anything which emits ink that is not an octopus.*
Socrates	*I don't think we'll find that in the dictionary. Isn't there a better definition?*

Glossary

Key terms

ACT UTILITARIAN *see* UTILITARIAN

ACTS AND OMISSIONS The theory that there is a moral difference between doing something, an *act*, and not doing something, an *omission*, even when the intentions and consequences are identical. For example, according to this theory, giving someone a fatal injection is morally different (worse) than not feeding them, though both, intentionally, result in death. Recognised in law, upheld by many religious faiths and widely accepted as a genuine moral distinction.

ABSOLUTIST / ABSOLUTISM A prescriptive ethical theory that holds that some kinds of actions or intentions are intrinsically right and others are intrinsically wrong, irrespective of the consequences. Absolutism is often linked to deontological theories, and to religious ethics which incorporate the notion of an objective Moral Law.

AGENT / AGENCY *see* MORAL AGENT

APPLIED ETHICS *see* PRACTICAL ETHICS

ARTIFICIAL INTELLIGENCE (A.I.) Is it possible for machines to think – have they got Artificial Intelligence? Some philosophers have argued that they can think, but only up to a point, and certainly not like human beings. Since computers cannot dream, fall in love, feel pain, etc., they are not conscious beings as humans are. If computers with consciousness could be developed, they would have artificial intelligence. Other philosophers have suggested that if computers could perform as well as humans in a variety of intelligence tests, then we would have to describe them as thinking things.

AUTONOMY The capacity to make decisions and moral choices for oneself. Some philosophers have argued that autonomy arises because we can make rational decisions concerning our natural desires and resist change those desires. If you simply follow your natural desires at every moment, then you are failing to be autonomous.

CONSEQUENTIALIST / CONSEQUENTIALISM A type of prescriptive ethical theory which holds that actions are good or bad solely according to their consequences or probable consequences. For example, if an action increases suffering, then it is a bad act whatever the motive, although the person doing the act is not necessarily to blame. If the action decreases suffering or increases happiness then it is a good act. Utilitarianism is a form of consequentialism.

DEONTOLOGICAL A type of prescriptive ethical theory which holds that certain actions should or shouldn't be done because they are right or wrong in themselves. With this theory consequences are irrelevant, since what matters is doing an action because we have an obligation to do it. Most religious codes of behaviour are deontological, as are the moral maxims of Immanuel Kant.

DIALECTICAL / DIALECTIC This was a form of debate popularised in ancient Greece by Plato in his Socratic dialogues. *See also* ELENCHUS.

DETERMINED / DETERMINISM The opposite of free will or freedom of choice. The belief that all events, including human actions, are caused, predetermined or inevitable. According to this theory, free will is an illusion, although many determinists are prepared to acknowledge that there is a significant (moral) difference between an action that we are forced to do and an action that is the result of some desire we have.

DUTY *see* OBLIGATION

ELENCHUS An ancient Greek term that means testing the strength of an argument or point of view. In Plato's early dialogues, Socrates uses this type of analysis to undermine his opponents' theories. Using a method of question and answer, Socrates gets his rivals to reveal a belief they have, and then later on, through argument, forces them to admit that they hold another belief that totally contradicts the first. This shows the incoherence of their beliefs, and enables Socrates to put forward his own theory as the stronger one.

ENDS *see* MEANS AND ENDS

END-IN-ITSELF *see* MEANS AND ENDS

ETHICS The study of how you ought to live and how you should act. Philosophers tend to use the terms *ethics* and *moral philosophy* interchangeably. *See also* PRESCRIPTIVE ETHICS and APPLIED ETHICS

EUDAIMONIA / EUDAIMON *Eudaimonia* is an ancient Greek term often translated as *happiness*. It is used by Plato and Aristotle to describe the life we all want to have. Although it is often translated as *happiness*, it is better understood as *flourishing*. So someone who is *eudaimon* is doing well in their life, living up to their potential, having a good life.

HEDONISM / HEDONISTIC The belief that our lives should be focused on achieving pleasure. *Psychological hedonism* is the theory that all our actions are aimed at producing pleasure. In other words, it would be impossible to perform an act that was not aimed at pleasure. Utilitarianism relies on a form of hedonism by suggesting that we ought to maximise pleasure for everyone because we all want pleasure.

MATERIALIST / MATERIALISM The view that everything that exists is made of physical matter. This effectively rules out the existence of any mysterious spiritual aspect to the universe, and attempts to explain any activity or event purely in terms of material causes and effects.

MEANS AND ENDS *Ends* (purposes, results) and *means* (ways of achieving them). These are often used together, as in 'The end justifies the means' or 'Always treat other people as ends in themselves, never as means to an end' (Immanuel Kant). For example, I put the kettle on, that is the *means* by which I make a cup of tea, the *end*. Some ends are also means to another goal, and drinking the tea might be a means to staying awake, or quenching my thirst. If, however, the end is done for its own sake then it is an *end-in-itself*.

MORAL AGENT Any being capable of moral action. An agent is someone who has the capacity to make choices and then to act upon those choices. *Moral agents* are thus able to think about their actions and then decide upon a particular course of action without being driven purely by biological instinct.

MORAL PATIENT A moral patient is anything that is the recipient of a moral action. We often think of patients in terms of rights and obligations. For example, if we have an obligation not to harm an animal (and it has a right not to be harmed), then it is a *moral patient*. How far we extend the concept of moral patient (do amoeba or insects have rights?) is a matter for debate.

MORAL RELATIVISM The belief that all moral judgements are relative to a person or culture. Relativists hold that there are no absolute facts about morality. Relativists may claim that moral statements have the same truth status as opinions concerning taste and beauty, or they may say that ethics is a matter of social convention.

MORALITY *see* PRESCRIPTIVE ETHICS

NECESSARY AND SUFFICIENT CONDITIONS *Necessary conditions* are those attributes without which X would not be an X. For example, it is necessary that for something to be a house it must be a building. Although it is necessary for a house to be a building, being a building is not sufficient to make something a house – more is required. *Sufficient conditions* are attributes which if possessed entail that X must be an X, for example, if a state has a queen, it must be a monarchy.

NORMATIVE *see* PRESCRIPTIVE

OBLIGATION or DUTY To be bound or required to do something, by contract or implicit agreement. An *obligation* may be a duty either to do something or to refrain from doing something. Obligations are linked to rights since if someone has a right to X, then I have an obligation either to help them to get X, or at least not to prevent them from getting X. Some philosophers, such as Kant, have argued that a morally good action is one that is done solely because it is my duty to do it and not because it will bring me any gain.

PATIENT *see* MORAL PATIENT

PRACTICAL ETHICS The application of prescriptive ethical theories to real-life problems such as abortion, war, animal rights, etc.

PRESCRIPTIVE ETHICS A theory that attempts to offer guidance or rules on how we should act. When we think of morality, or ethics in general, we are normally thinking of prescriptive ethics. Common *prescriptive theories* include Kant's moral theory and utilitarianism.

PROBLEM OF EVIL A problem that arises for religious believers. If God is all-knowing, all-powerful, and all-loving, then why does God allow pain and suffering to exist in the world? There have been many attempts to defend the existence of God against the problem of evil, and some philosophers feel that the problem is insurmountable.

QUALIA The particular experiences and sensations that all conscious beings are capable of having. For example, the taste of honey, the colour of a sunset, the feeling of pins and needles, etc.

RELATIVISM *see* MORAL RELATIVISM

RHETORICAL / RHETORIC The skill of public speaking and of winning an audience over to your argument. Plato was opposed to rhetoric (as it was practised by the Sophists) because it was not concerned with the truth but simply with persuading an audience of a particular viewpoint.

RIGHTS A person's or being's justified entitlements as a member of society. The justification is now commonly based on a contractual obligation, for example, to be protected from violence or to vote. (The *Universal Declaration of Human Rights* is a widely respected description of universal rights.) Jeremy Bentham once called the concept of *natural rights* 'nonsense upon stilts' and the propensity of many groups to claim they have a right (for example the right to party!) without showing what contractual obligation it is based upon, has meant that much talk of rights has been discredited.

RULE UTILITARIAN *see* UTILITARIAN

SLIPPERY SLOPE ARGUMENTS An informal type of argument aimed at showing that because there is a connection between two extremes, then accepting one extreme entails eventually accepting the other. In ethics, arguments like these are common and assume that if you allow one practice, you will inevitably allow other more objectionable moral practices. For example, a slippery slope argument might claim that if you permit abortion of fetuses up to one month, then you will have to permit infanticide too. In practice it is usually possible to draw a line between one kind of action and another by drawing on commonly agreed criteria.

SOCIAL CONTRACT The theory that stable societies are formed through the establishment of a contract whereby individuals agree to forgo some of their rights in exchange for a protective government. This is an imaginary device used by philosophers such as Hobbes to justify our moral obligations to the state, and to other individuals in society. Without this contract, society would be chaotic, those with the most violent tendencies would dominate, and our lives would be 'nasty, brutish and short'.

SOCRATIC DIALOGUE The name given to the early plays written by Plato in which the main character is Socrates. What characterises these dialogues is Socrates' insistent questioning of those around him about the nature of moral concepts. Plato used this method of question and answer as a way of refining our understanding of a concept, and perhaps of eventually reaching the truth about that concept.

SOPHISTS The name given to the disparate group of sages who wandered throughout the Greek world in the 5th century BCE. They were the forerunners of Socrates, Plato and Aristotle. Although they had no common doctrine, many believed there were no moral truths, all that mattered was doing well in life. They taught the art of rhetoric as a means to doing well in life – if you could persuade someone of anything then you would have the power to get what you wanted in life.

(Comparisons have been made with spin doctors and advertisers in the contemporary world.) It was this moral cynicism that Socrates and Plato most despised and reacted against.

SPECIESISM Term coined by contemporary philosopher, Peter Singer, to describe unjustified discrimination against another species, akin to racism, sexism, etc. Essentially it means treating only humans as genuine moral patients.

UNIVERSALISABILITY The theory that a right action is one that you can claim 'anyone in your position should have done'. In other words, a right action is one that you can universalise. For example: I might be trying to decide whether or not I should break my promise to take my nephew to the zoo. I should then ask myself, 'What would happen if everyone went around breaking promises?' Well, in that case no one would believe anyone's promises and promises would cease to mean anything, they would cease to exist. It is impossible to universalise breaking a promise without contradicting myself, therefore I ought to keep my promise.

UTILITY The usefulness of an action / event / object. In other words the capacity of the action / event / object to produce a desired result. In ethics this result would be one that promotes the interests or happiness of society. Utilitarians believe that a morally good action is one that maximises utility, i.e. produces the greatest amount of happiness.

UTILITARIANISM / UTILITARIANS An ethical theory, refined by John Stuart Mill, that tells us how we ought and ought not to behave. Utilitarianism is a consequentialist ethic. The theory of utilitarianism is deceptively simple, based on 'the greatest happiness' principle:

A good action is one that maximises general happiness or minimises pain.
A bad action is one that maximises general pain or minimises happiness.

Utilitarians believe that we all desire happiness and we all dislike genuine suffering. The more happiness and less suffering there is in the world generally, then the better the world is. So we should all try to act in a way that makes the world happier and avoid acting in ways that increase general suffering. Utilitarians think that this simple principle lies behind all the other ethical systems in the world. Lying, stealing, killing, are all bad if they cause suffering and reduce the happiness in the world.

There is a difference between act utilitarianism and rule utilitarianism. *Act utilitarians* think that we should maximise happiness by assessing the consequences of each new situation. However, this leads to a number of problems, in particular working out what the consequences of each action will be. *Rule utilitarians* get round this by suggesting that we should maximise happiness by following certain rules of thumb which have been shown to maximise happiness in the past. Whatever form it takes, utilitarianism is one of the most discussed ethical theories in the world. The theory has become infused into various areas of our lives, and lies behind many government policies and departmental calculations.

Key names

ARISTOTLE (384–322 BCE) Ancient Greek philosopher. As the pupil of Plato, Aristotle refined his teacher's ideas, rejecting Plato's theory of a perfect world of forms and developing a philosophy based on the study of this world. He established the first rules of logic, and wrote widely on every academic subject, eventually founding his own university, the Lyceum, as a rival to Plato's Academy. In ethics he is most famous for arguing that eudaimonia is what we all aim for in life, and the way to achieve it is by fulfilling our function as humans, i.e. by reasoning. Like Plato he was much more concerned with encouraging people to develop good characters, than he was in constructing a theory about right and wrong actions.

BENTHAM, JEREMY (1748–1832) English philosopher. Bentham is considered the father of utilitarianism. His *Introduction to the Principles of Morals and Legislation* (1789) is a classic text concerning putting utilitarian principles into action in government and the law. Bentham's version of utilitarianism was simple: an action is good if overall it maximises the pleasure and minimises the pain of those it affects.

DARWIN, CHARLES (1809–1882) English scientist. Darwin's *On the Origin of Species* (1859) introduced the idea of evolution by natural selection, establishing it as an explanation for the diversity of species and their adaptations to the environment. Although the theory has been refined by subsequent generations, it has not been superseded, and has been enormously influential, not least on the decline of literalist religious beliefs.

DAWKINS, RICHARD (1941) Best-selling author of *The Selfish Gene* (1976) and Professor of the Public Understanding of Science at Oxford University, he has done much to popularise a Darwinian view of evolution, human behaviour and morality.

HOBBES, THOMAS (1588–1679) English philosopher. Hobbes grew up to witness the revolt against the monarchy that became the English Civil War. As a result, his moral and political philosophy, as expressed in the *Leviathan* (1651), was concerned with establishing reasons why we should obey the state, and thus avoid the horrors of civil war. He was a fearful man, and believed that all humans were essentially selfish – the only reason why we are moral at all is because it is in our own interests to avoid the consequences of a 'state of nature', i.e. a world without laws. What Hobbes managed to do was to provide a plausible account of how morality can have a foundation independent of any religious or metaphysical beliefs.

KANT, IMMANUEL (1724–1804) German philosopher. Kant believed that we should think before we act. He thought that we could always work out the right course of action by reasoning about the problem. He suggested a way of thinking, a formula, that would enable us to work out how to do the right thing. When we think that we have done a right action what we mean is that we think that anyone else in the same situation should also have acted in the same way. Kant believed that as rational beings we should only act in a way that we could genuinely apply to all people: 'Act only on that maxim which you can at the same time will to become a universal law.' This is known as Kant's categorical imperative (*See also* UNIVERSALISABILITY).

Mill, John Stuart (1806–1703) English philosopher. Wrote on utilitarianism, freedom, and women's rights, amongst other things. His argument, in *On Liberty* (1859), that the state is only justified in restricting the freedom of the individual to prevent harm to others, has been an important influence on liberal thinking. Mill's version of utilitarianism differed from his teacher Bentham's insofar as Mill distinguished between different kinds of pleasures ('higher' and 'lower') some of which were more valuable than others.

Plato (c.428–347 BCE) Ancient Greek philosopher. As one modern philosopher said, all philosophy is a footnote to Plato. Although there had been philosophers in Ancient Greece before Plato, he was the first to attempt a systematic account of all the philosophical problems that had been raised. In doing so he established the western philosophical tradition of the analysis of arguments and the construction of theories based on justified reasoning. His early works are written as plays which centre around the narrator, Socrates, (Plato's teacher). In these plays Socrates discusses the nature of morality with a variety of distinguished characters. In his later years he founded the first university in the west, the Academy in Athens, and was Aristotle's teacher.

Rawls, John (1921) American philosopher. Rawls' *A Theory of Justice* (1971) expands on social contract theory by suggesting that the concept of justice be based on a hypothetical discussion in an 'original position' of equality. In this original position there is a 'veil of ignorance' drawn over the participants so that they know nothing about themselves: their social position, health, wealth, etc. All self-interest is eliminated from the debate. Rawls asks us to imagine what concept of justice the participants would arrive at. He believed that the resulting concept would be one of fairness and equality – we would seek to preserve liberty and a reasonable standard of living for all.

Singer, Peter (1946) Australian philosopher interested in ethics of life and death situations, and animal rights. A contemporary utilitarian, who has extended the theory to include non-human animals, *see* SPECIESISM.

Socrates (c.470–399 BCE) Ancient Greek philosopher. Socrates provided the impetus that led to the establishing of the western philosophical tradition by his pupil Plato. However, he wrote nothing himself, confining himself to debates and discussions with fellow philosophers and sophists. What we know about him is only through the writings of his contemporaries, the dialogues of Plato, and the references of Aristotle. The figure of Socrates as presented to us by Plato is of a modest man, with a sharp mind and tongue, dedicated to weeding out the inconsistencies in the beliefs of others. He often claimed that he was ignorant (or at least only wise insofar as he didn't pretend to know anything) and was simply interested in scrutinising the views of others. In 399 BCE he was arrested and sentenced to death by the Athenian government. It was his trial and final hours of life that were depicted in two of Plato's first dialogues, the *Apology* and the *Phaedo*.

Appendix 1
Ethical currency units

For activities 11 and 12

Photocopy each denomination onto a different coloured paper.

AN EYE FOR AN EYE AN EYE FOR AN EYE AN EYE FOR AN EYE AN EYE FOR AN EYE AN EYE

 **5000** *ECUs*
Five Thousand Ethical Currency Units

WOULD MAKE THE WORLD BLIND WOULD MAKE THE WORLD BLIND WOULD MAKE THE

AN EYE FOR AN EYE AN EYE FOR AN EYE AN EYE FOR AN EYE AN EYE FOR AN EYE AN EYE

 **5000** *ECUs*
Five Thousand Ethical Currency Units

WOULD MAKE THE WORLD BLIND WOULD MAKE THE WORLD BLIND WOULD MAKE THE

AN EYE FOR AN EYE AN EYE FOR AN EYE AN EYE FOR AN EYE AN EYE FOR AN EYE AN EYE

 **5000** *ECUs*
Five Thousand Ethical Currency Units

WOULD MAKE THE WORLD BLIND WOULD MAKE THE WORLD BLIND WOULD MAKE THE

AN EYE FOR AN EYE AN EYE FOR AN EYE AN EYE FOR AN EYE AN EYE FOR AN EYE AN EYE

 **5000** *ECUs*
Five Thousand Ethical Currency Units

WOULD MAKE THE WORLD BLIND WOULD MAKE THE WORLD BLIND WOULD MAKE THE

Photocopy each denomination onto a different coloured paper.

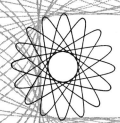
TREAT OTHERS TREAT OTHERS TREAT OTHERS TREAT OTHERS TREAT OTHERS TREAT OTHERS

2000 ECUs
Two Thousand Ethical Currency Units

AS YOU WANT TO BE TREATED AS YOU WANT TO BE TREATED AS YOU WANT TO BE TREATED

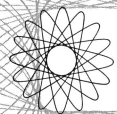
TREAT OTHERS TREAT OTHERS TREAT OTHERS TREAT OTHERS TREAT OTHERS TREAT OTHERS

2000 ECUs
Two Thousand Ethical Currency Units

AS YOU WANT TO BE TREATED AS YOU WANT TO BE TREATED AS YOU WANT TO BE TREATED

TREAT OTHERS TREAT OTHERS TREAT OTHERS TREAT OTHERS TREAT OTHERS TREAT OTHERS

2000 ECUs
Two Thousand Ethical Currency Units

AS YOU WANT TO BE TREATED AS YOU WANT TO BE TREATED AS YOU WANT TO BE TREATED

TREAT OTHERS TREAT OTHERS TREAT OTHERS TREAT OTHERS TREAT OTHERS TREAT OTHERS

2000 ECUs
Two Thousand Ethical Currency Units

AS YOU WANT TO BE TREATED AS YOU WANT TO BE TREATED AS YOU WANT TO BE TREATED

Photocopy each denomination onto a different coloured paper.

MAXIMISE HAPPINESS MAXIMISE HAPPINESS MAXIMISE HAPPINESS MAXIMISE HAPPINESS

1000 ECUs

One Thousand Ethical Currency Units

MINIMISE PAIN MINIMISE PAIN MINIMISE PAIN MINIMISE PAIN MINIMISE PAIN MINIMISE PAIN

MAXIMISE HAPPINESS MAXIMISE HAPPINESS MAXIMISE HAPPINESS MAXIMISE HAPPINESS

1000 ECUs

One Thousand Ethical Currency Units

MINIMISE PAIN MINIMISE PAIN MINIMISE PAIN MINIMISE PAIN MINIMISE PAIN MINIMISE PAIN

MAXIMISE HAPPINESS MAXIMISE HAPPINESS MAXIMISE HAPPINESS MAXIMISE HAPPINESS

1000 ECUs

One Thousand Ethical Currency Units

MINIMISE PAIN MINIMISE PAIN MINIMISE PAIN MINIMISE PAIN MINIMISE PAIN MINIMISE PAIN

MAXIMISE HAPPINESS MAXIMISE HAPPINESS MAXIMISE HAPPINESS MAXIMISE HAPPINESS

1000 ECUs

One Thousand Ethical Currency Units

MINIMISE PAIN MINIMISE PAIN MINIMISE PAIN MINIMISE PAIN MINIMISE PAIN MINIMISE PAIN

Appendix 2
Useful reading

This bibliography includes suggestions for further reading in ethics. The asterisked (*) titles are recommended as useful introductions to the subject for the non-specialist.

General introductions to ethics

MacIntyre, A. *A Short History of Ethics*, Routledge, 1967.
Singer, P. *A Companion to Ethics** Basil Blackwell, 1991.
Vardy, P. *The Puzzle of Ethics* Fount, 1994.
Williams, B. *Morality, an Introduction to Ethics** Cambridge University Press, 1972.

Practical and applied ethics

Beauchamp, T.L. and Childress, J.F. *Principles of Biomedical Ethics* Oxford University Press, 1989.
Glover, J. *Causing Death and Saving Lives** Penguin, 1977.
Hirsthouse, R. *Humans and Other Animals* Open University Press, 1999.
Lockwood, M. *Moral Dilemmas in Modern Medicine* Oxford University Press, 1985.
Singer, P. (ed.) *Applied Ethics** Oxford University Press, 1986.
Singer, P. *Practical Ethics* Cambridge University Press, 1993.

Historical texts and prescriptive ethics

Bentham, J. (ed. Warnock, M.) *Introduction to the Principles of Morals and Legislation* Fontana, 1973.
Hobbes, T. (ed. Plamenatz, J.) *Leviathan* Collins, 1972.
Hume, D. (ed. Beauchamp, T.) *An Enquiry Concerning the Principles of Morals* Oxford University Press, 1998.
Mill, J.S. (ed. Warnock, M.) *Utilitarianism and Other Essays* Fontana, 1973.
Paton, H.J. *The Moral Law* Hutchinson, 1953.
Plato, *The Republic* Penguin, 1986.
Plato, *Gorgias* Oxford University Press, 1994.
Rawls, J. *A Theory of Justice* Oxford University Press, 1972.
Sartre, J-P. *Existentialism and Humanism* Methuen, 1987.
Smart, J.J.C. and Williams, B. *Utilitarianism: For and Against** Cambridge University Press, 1973.
Urmson, J. *Aristotle's Ethics* Oxford University Press, 1988.

Meta-ethics

Foot, P. *Theories of Ethics* Oxford University Press,1967.
Harman, G. *The Nature of Morality* Oxford University Press, 1977.
Mackie, J.L. *Ethics: Inventing Right and Wrong* Penguin, 1977.
Warnock, M. *Ethics since 1900* Oxford University Press, 1960.
Williams, B. *Ethics and the Limits of Philosophy** Fontana, 1985.

Activity-centred teaching

Bruner, J.S. *Towards a Theory of Instruction* Harvard University Press, 1962.
Goodman, F.L. 'An introduction to the virtues of gaming' in Tansey, P.J. (ed.) *Educational Aspects of Simulation* McGraw Hill, 1971.
Greenblat, C.S. and Duke, R.D. *Principles and Practice of Gaming Simulations* Sage Publications Ltd., 1981.
Jones, G. and Hayward, J. 'Goodbye chalk and talk' in *The Philosophers' Magazine* TPM Issue 10, Spring 2000.
Miami University, *Teaching Philosophy*, journal published by Miami University, Ohio.
Morton, A. *Philosophy in Practice* Blackwell Publishers, 1996.
Taylor and Walford, *Learning and the Simulation Game* Open University Press, 1978.
Wilson, A. *Demonstrating Philosophy* University Press of America, 1989.